Phrasal Movement and Its Kin

Linguistic Inquiry Monographs
Samuel Jay Keyser, general editor

Phrasal Movement and Its Kin

David Pesetsky

The MIT Press
Cambridge, Massachusetts
London, England

This book was set in Times New Roman on '3B2' by Asco Typesetters, Hong Kong and was printed and bound in the United States of America.

Library of Congress Cataloging-in-Publication Data

Pesetsky, David Michael.
  Phrasal movement and its kin / David Pesetsky.
    p.   cm. — (Linguistic inquiry monographs ; 37)
  Includes bibliographical references and index.
  ISBN 0-262-16196-6 (hc. : alk. paper) — ISBN 0-262-66166-7 (pbk. : alk. paper)
  1. Grammar, Comparative and general—Syntax. 2. Phraseology. 3. Grammar, Comparative and general—Interrogative. 4. Generative grammar. I. Title. II. Series.
P296.P48   2000
415—dc21   00-038695

Contents

Series Foreword

We are pleased to present the thirty-seventh in the series *Linguistic Inquiry Monographs*. These monographs present new and original research beyond the scope of the article. We hope they will benefit our field by bringing to it perspectives that will stimulate further research and insight.

Originally published in limited edition, the *Linguistic Inquiry Monographs* are now more widely available. This change is due to the great interest engendered by the series and by the needs of a growing readership. The editors thank the readers for their support and welcome suggestions about future directions for the series.

Samuel Jay Keyser
for the Editorial Board

Preface

The investigations reported here are the result of three lucky events. The first occurred in 1986. I had recently done the work reported in Pesetsky 1987, and I received in the mail a copy of É. Kiss 1986. Since I had argued at length that D-linked *wh*-phrases do not display Superiority effects, I was astonished by a paradigm reported by É. Kiss, which appears here as example (98). These facts remained stubbornly in my mind for the next decade as an unsolved puzzle. É. Kiss did not publish her paper in the form that I received—and, in fact, did not even recall discovering the crucial facts when she heard this work presented as a talk in 1998. But the facts are hers nonetheless.

The second lucky event occurred in the spring of 1994. I had just taught Pesetsky 1987 in a graduate syntax class, but had not assigned a problem set on it. The next topic on the syllabus was antecedent-contained deletion, which I was teaching for the first time. I needed a problem set that covered both topics, and it occurred to me that perhaps Pesetsky 1987 might make a prediction about antecedent-contained deletion in *wh*-phrases that should have moved overtly but didn't—a prediction that might serve as the topic of a single, unified problem set on the two topics. The result was the observation in (60) and (61). A conversation with Chris Kennedy (who had been thinking about this issue independently) reinforced my interest in this contrast.

Finally, in 1996 I was lucky enough to hear a presentation of Beck 1996 and Beck and Kim 1996 by Sigrid Beck at an informal meeting of MIT's student-organized LF Reading Group. Her observations immediately reminded me of É. Kiss's observations. This book grew out of my attempt to understand the connection between these two sets of observations—an effort that led me right back to the data from my problem set on antecedent-contained deletion.

My proposals have undergone several transformations, with the result that some whose comments are acknowledged in this work may not recognize it as the descendent of the one that they heard. I am grateful to those with whom I discussed the work during its various stages, and to those who commented on public presentations. The earliest versions were presented in the spring of 1997 in a seminar at MIT and in a colloquium at the University of Pittsburgh. A version more similar to this book, but couched in an Optimality Theory setting (see note 57), was presented in a course at the 1997 LSA Summer Institute at Cornell University. For helpful questions and discussion, I am especially grateful to Jonathan Bobaljik, Barbara Citko, Peter Cole, Molly Diesing, Gabriella Hermon, Satoshi Tomioka, Colin Wilson, and Susanne Wurmbrand. This version was also presented at the conference "Colloque de Syntaxe et Sémantique" held at Université de Paris VII in October 1997.

Especially important was the opportunity to present the work once more at MIT during the fall of 1997, at which time the role of feature movement fell into place. For crucial discussion during this period, I am grateful to Elena Anagnostopoulou, Sigrid Beck, Michael Brody, Noam Chomsky, Michel DeGraff, Kai von Fintel, Danny Fox, Paul Hagstrom, Irene Heim, Sabine Iatridou, Roumyana Izvorski, Shigeru Miyagawa, Jonathan Nissenbaum, Norvin Richards (whose work also inspired the research reported here), and Uli Sauerland. This version was presented as a talk during the 1997–1998 academic year at the University of Massachusetts at Amherst, the University of Maryland, the University of São Paulo, and Sophia University, and at the conferences "Formal Approaches to Slavic Linguistics" (University of Washington), "Perfection in Syntax" (Collegium Budapest), and "Eastern States Conference on Linguistics (ESCOL)" (Yale University). More extended presentations at the University of Brasilia and at Kanda University (Makuhari Kaihin, Japan) during the summer of 1998 played an important role in clarifying the ideas and teaching me the best ways to present them. For their challenging questions and helpful comments, I thank both the audience in Brasilia (among others, Lucia Lobato, Rozana Naves, Cilene Rodrigues, Heloisa Salles, and Clovis Santos) and the audience at Kanda University, among many others Nobuko Hasegawa, Kazuko Inoue, Yasu Ishii, Noriko Kawasaki, Hisatsugu Kitahara, Mari Takahashi, and Keiko Yoshida). A final presentation at the University of Vienna in June 1999 helped with the discussion of German. Thanks as well to Roumyana Izvorski for information about Bulgarian, and to the German-speaking linguists at MIT for invaluable assistance with "Beck effects" and other matters.

The first draft of this book was written in July and August 1998. Michael Brody, Kai von Fintel, Günther Grewendorf, Paul Hagstrom, Sabine Iatridou, and Norvin Richards provided useful comments on this draft. Special thanks to Shigeru Miyagawa for crucial encouragement and assistance as I wrote it. Three anonymous reviewers for MIT Press also provided helpful and thought-provoking comments that improved many parts of the book. Almost all their suggestions have been taken into account here. Thanks also to Anne Mark for her editorial assistance.

Chapter 1

Introduction

This book is an attempt to discover the types of movement and movement-like relations that link positions in syntactic structure. I will argue that we can identify at least two kinds of movement-like relations: phrasal movement of the traditional kind, and the relation that Chomsky (1995) has called "feature movement."[1] My results differ sharply from Chomsky's, however, in supporting an additional distinction between overt and covert phrasal movement. If these conclusions are correct, then "feature movement" is not the proper reanalysis of covert phrasal movement, as Chomsky suggests, but is a phenomenon in its own right—a type of syntactic relation distinct from previously studied instances of movement. All in all, then, we will see evidence for three kinds of movement relations: overt phrasal movement, covert phrasal movement, and feature movement.

The focus of the book will be *wh*-questions. In particular, the classification of movement-like relations will allow us to understand the story behind *wh*-questions, in which an otherwise inviolable property of movement—"Attract Closest"—appears to be violated. I will show that Attract Closest is actually *not* violated in the cases in question. The key to this conclusion will be a demonstration that more movement takes place in these configurations than one might suspect, so that the "closest" element is really being attracted after all. Crucially, this conclusion is possible only in light of the expanded repertoire of movement-like relations presented in this book.

The book concludes with a corollary investigation of a semantic restriction on *wh*-questions investigated by Beck (1996). This restriction appears in English in exactly those constructions examined in chapters 2–4, but it has a wider distribution in German—and an even wider distribution in Japanese and Korean. I will show that the distribution of Beck's effect in these three language types follows straightforwardly from my hypothesis about the movement-like relations available to languages, in tandem with a typology of specifier requirements that also figures prominently in chapters 2–4. In short, I will argue that my general view of movement helps explain how the syntax of *wh*-questions differs across languages.

I begin with an introduction to the central issues of the book.

1.1   Phrasal Movement: Overt and Covert

The term *movement* describes a situation in which a syntactic unit—for example, a phrase—appears to occupy more than one position in syntactic structure. Movement is most easily detected when a word or phrase is pronounced in a position where we do not expect it to be pronounced (given an independently well motivated syntax for argument taking and modification). Often, when a word or phrase is pronounced in an "unexpected" position, it is pronounced *only* in the unexpected position;[2] it is not additionally pronounced in its expected ("trace") position. As observed in the early 1970s, the pronunciation position in these cases typically c-commands the trace position. This constellation of syntactic and phonological properties constitutes what we can call *overt phrasal movement*.[3]

Overt phrasal movement is *movement* in that it obeys a characteristic set of command restrictions, as well as locality conditions governing the distance between the "expected" position and the position created by movement. It is *phrasal* in that the moved unit is a word or group of words. (Reconstruction effects reveal the presence of the moved phrase in both trace position and targeted position.) It is *overt* in that it affects the phonology; the sentence sounds different with the movement operation than it would have sounded without it. Many of the best-studied instances of movement belong to the category of overt phrasal movement. Of special interest here will be overt *wh*-phrase movement of the sort familiar from many languages, including English.

Overt wh-*phrase movement*
(1) Which book did Mary give _____ to Sue?

As linguists, we are lucky that overt phrasal movement exists; if it did not, movement itself might not have been discovered. Nonetheless, from a broader perspective, the pronunciation pattern of overt phrasal movement seems rather arbitrary. Why should pronunciation target the moved position and not the trace position? Why not the other way around, for example? In fact, a large body of research shows that other pronunciation patterns do exist. For example, Chomsky (1976), May (1977, 1985), and Huang (1981, 1982) provided central arguments for the existence of alternative pronunciation patterns for movement. These researchers argued that sometimes a moved element is pronounced in a trace position, rather than in its final (highest) position. This type of movement is traditionally called *covert*. Here I will call it *covert phrasal movement*. Covert phrasal movement is *movement* insofar as it creates a link between positions that obeys command restrictions and islands in a manner familiar from overt phrasal movement. Covert phrasal movement is *covert* in that it does not affect the segmental phonology. The moved words affected by covert phrasal movement are pronounced just as if no movement had taken place. Covert phrasal movement is *phrasal* in that entire words and word groups are copied from the trace position to the new position.

A particularly good argument for covert phrasal movement comes from "antecedent-contained" anaphora of the sort familiar from research on antecedent-contained deletion (ACD) constructions like (2) (Bouton 1970; Sag 1976; May 1985; Larson and May 1990).

ACD
(2) Mary [$_{VP}$ invited [$_{DP}$ everyone that I did [$_{VP}$ Δ]]].

The argument runs as follows. The example in (2) most naturally has the interpretation in (3) (where *t* is the trace of relativization within DP).

Interpretation of ellipsis in (2)
(3) Mary [$_{VP}$ invited [$_{DP}$ everyone that I [$_{VP}$ invited t]]].

It is a fact about VP-ellipsis (Hankamer and Sag 1976) that unlike a pronoun, which may take its reference from a contextually salient but unmentioned individual, an elided VP requires a linguistic expression—a pronounced VP—as its antecedent. Thus, although I can say "Thank goodness *he*'s left" as a response to the departure of a salient but unmentioned individual, I cannot say "Thank goodness *I* didn't [$_{VP}$ Δ]" as a response to someone's tripping over a wire. Consequently, the fact that the elided VP in (3) is understood as the expression *invited t* tells us that the linguistic context must contain an antecedent of the form *invited t*. If the analysis of (2) does not involve covert movement, then we cannot understand the availability of interpretation (3). Without covert movement, (2) contains no VP of the form *invited t*—only a VP of the form *invited everyone that I did*. But if the phrase *everyone that I did* undergoes covert phrasal movement to a VP-external position, then it leaves behind a VP of the form *invited t*, supplying the appropriate antecedent for the elided VP.

Example (2) after covert phrasal movement
(4) [$_{DP}$ everyone that I [$_{VP}$ invited t]] [Mary [$_{VP}$ invited t]]

Support for this proposal comes from Larson and May's (1990) discussion of configurations in which both a higher and a lower VP can serve as antecedent for an instance of ACD (a discussion anticipated by Sag (1976, 72–74)). Larson and May note that the higher VP can be chosen only if the phrase containing the ACD is interpreted with scope wider than the higher VP. The phenomenon is demonstrated in (5).[4]

Scope/ellipsis correlations
(5) a. John refused to visit [every city Mary did [$_{VP}$ Δ]].
    b. i. John refused to visit [every city Mary visited t].   [ambiguous: compatible with narrow or wide scope of *every city*]
       ii. John refused to visit [every city Mary *refused to visit t*]. [unambiguous: incompatible with narrow scope of *every city*]

The story is more complex than this, of course, if traces are simply the originals of which moved phrases are copies (Chomsky 1993). In the process of semantic interpretation, descriptive material in the trace position must be deleted, so that the trace not only functions as a variable, but also helps provide an appropriate antecedent VP for the ellipsis site. Fox (1995), building on a discussion by Fiengo and May (1994), shows that this process (which, he argues, is motivated by ACD interpretation) interacts with Principle C of the binding theory just as expected. Covert movement in normal circumstances is insufficient to bleed Principle C (presumably because nothing motivates deletion of the trace-internal material that generates the Principle C violation).

No bleeding of Principle C without ACD
(6) *I [sent him$_i$ [every letter that John$_i$ expected I would write t]].

Covert movement with ACD, however, requires deletion of the trace-internal material, which in turn removes the Principle C violation.

Bleeding of Principle C with ACD
(7) I [sent him$_i$ [every letter that John$_i$ expected I would [$_{VP}$ Δ]] →
    [every letter that John$_i$ expected I would [$_{VP}$ send him$_i$ t]] I [sent him$_i$ t]

Important complications are discussed by Fox (1995, 1998) and Sauerland (1998b) and will be glossed over here. Some of these complications concern the landing site of covert movement in cases like (2) and (7)—that is, whether the relevant DP moves to an IP-initial position, as shown in (4) and (7), or to some other (perhaps lower) VP-external position, as Fox argues. The only point relevant here is the fundamental conclusion that the interpretation of ACD requires phonologically vacuous (i.e., covert) movement of the phrase that contains the deletion site.

Covert phrasal movement has often been viewed as a language- or construction-specific variant of overt phrasal movement. For example, many researchers have proposed covert phrasal movement of *wh*-phrases to C as a covert version of the overt phrasal *wh*-movement displayed in (1) (e.g., Huang 1981, 1982; Aoun, Hornstein, and Sportiche 1981). Covert *wh*-movement has frequently been proposed for languages like Chinese and Japanese (where most *wh*-phrases are pronounced in situ) as well for *wh*-in-situ in multiple questions in languages like English. One argument for covert *wh*-movement in English multiple questions can be constructed from the fact that both overt and (putative) covert *wh*-movement obey the same command condition. The trace position must be c-commanded by the C to which the *wh*-phrase moves.

Command condition on overt and covert wh-*movement*
(8) a.   [Give a book to John] I can guess [who C will ____]!   [cf. *I can guess who will give a book to John!*]
   b.   *[Give a book to t$_i$] I can guess [who$_i$ C Mary will ____]!   [cf. *I can guess who Mary will give a book to!*]
   c.   *[Give a book to whom] I can guess [who C will ____]!   [cf. *I can guess who will give a book to whom!*]

The ungrammaticality of (8b) and (8c) probably reflects a command requirement on movement (rather than, for example, a semantic condition on variable binding), since no similar condition affects pronouns when they function as bound variables, as (9) demonstrates. The semantics, at least, can apparently inspect a fronted VP in its (reconstructed) base position.[5]

Command condition is not semantic
(9) [Give a book to his$_i$ mother] I can guess who will ____!

If these conclusions are correct, the LF representation of *Who gave what to whom?* may look something like (10b), in which *wh*-movement has affected all three *wh*-elements. Overstriking indicates the pronunciation pattern.

English multiple questions: LF and pronunciation
(10) a. Who gave what to whom?
     b. [who ~~what whom~~ [~~who~~ gave *what* to *whom*]][6]

As often noted in the 1980s (Lasnik and Saito 1984; Rudin 1985; Pesetsky 1987), this hypothesis about multiple questions in English is supported by the behavior of multiple questions in Slavic languages. (I focus here on Bulgarian.) In these languages the covert instances of *wh*-movement posited for English are overt. That is, if (10b) represents a correct analysis for English multiple questions, it differs from its Bulgarian counterpart (11b) only in how its *wh*-chains are pronounced.

Bulgarian multiple questions: LF and pronunciation
(11) a. Koj kakvo na kogo dade?
        who what to whom gave
        'Who gave what to whom?'
     b. [koj kakvo na kogo [~~koj~~ dade ~~kakvo na kogo~~]]

Of course, if covert *wh*-movement in English truly mirrors overt *wh*-movement, it should be demonstrably *phrasal*. That is, we should have evidence that covert *wh*-movement copies word groups similar to those copied in overt movement. ACD provides a test for this prediction. English *wh*-phrases pronounced in situ may contain an instance of ACD. This fact supports the hypothesis that *wh*-phrases may undergo covert phrasal movement, though it leaves open for now the possibility that the covert phrasal movement that resolves ACD is not *wh*-movement (as argued by Hornstein (1994, 1995) and Lasnik (1993), among others). I return to this issue in section 3.2, where I argue that the movement that resolves ACD is indeed *wh*-movement. ((12c) is from Fiengo and May 1994, 242.)

ACD licensed in wh-*in-situ*
(12) a. Which girl invited [which student that John did [$_{VP}$ Δ]]?
     b. I need to know who can speak [which languages that Ken Hale can [$_{VP}$ Δ]]?
     c. Which spy-master suspected which spy that Angleton did [$_{VP}$ Δ]]?

Let us now consider the mechanics of covert phrasal movement in more detail. Traditionally, the pronunciation difference between overt and covert phrasal movement has been viewed as a consequence of the timing of movement within a derivational model. In the model assumed in many studies—the so-called (inverted) Y-model of Chomsky and Lasnik (1977) —the pronunciation of the chains of positions linked by movement is governed by a simple principle of Phonological Spell-Out.

Phonological Spell-Out in the Y-model
(13) Pronounce only the highest position in a movement chain.

On this view, covert movement is simply movement that takes place after Spell-Out. Movement after Spell-Out thus creates a situation in which the highest position at LF is higher than the highest position at the time of Spell-Out. Phonological processing and covert movement take place on separate derivational tracks (the arms of the inverted "Y"). Though this view is common, few (if any) sustainable arguments seem to support the Y-model's segregation of overt and covert movement within the syntax. Indeed, the segregation of overt and covert movement into separate blocks of structure-building operations creates complications for simple views of structure building like that advanced by Chomsky (1993, 1995), in which the phrase structure of an expression simply *is* its derivational history. Covert movement as analyzed within the Y-model would be fairly unique in "altering the historical record"—by tinkering with the internal structure of the derivation.

In Pesetsky 1997, 1998, I suggested an alternative view, which places the burden of accounting for the covert/overt distinction on the phonology. (Similar ideas have been developed by Bobaljik (1995), who calls this view *single-output syntax*, and by Groat and O'Neil (1996). A precursor was Brody 1995, circulated in 1992.) In this view the syntax is simpler than in the Y-model; there is just one movement component. The trade-off comes in the phonological component, where the simple principle of Phonological Spell-Out in (13) is replaced by phonological principles of chain pronunciation that regulate the pronunciation of moved elements in a more complex manner. These principles determine, for example, whether the head of a chain is the only position pronounced (overt phrasal movement) or whether a trace position will be pronounced instead (covert phrasal movement). An indirect but telling argument for this point of view was the observation that the dichotomy "overt versus covert" inherent in the Y-model is too crude, since there are other pronunciation patterns for chains. Sometimes no position within a chain is pronounced, and sometimes more than one chain position is pronounced (e.g., in resumptive pronoun constructions).

In this study very little will depend on the choice between the Y-model and single-output syntax.[7] Nonetheless, the overall picture will be significantly easier to discuss within the architecturally simpler single-output model. I will therefore assume that there is only one cycle of syntactic movement, and I will describe pronunciation distinctions like the one between overt and covert phrasal movement as essentially phonological. Against this backdrop I will argue that (14) and (15) properly characterize the difference between English and Bulgarian pronunciation patterns in multiple questions. Reference to the "first instance" and "secondary instances" of *wh*-movement will be justified shortly.

Pronunciation rule (English)
(14) a. The first instance of *wh*-phrase movement to C is *overt*, in that *wh* is pronounced in its new position and unpronounced in its trace positions.
    b. Secondary instances of *wh*-phrase movement to C are *covert*, in that *wh* is pronounced in its trace position and unpronounced in its new position.

Pronunciation rule (Bulgarian)
(15) All *wh*-phrase movement to C is *overt,* in that *wh* is pronounced in its new position and unpronounced in its trace positions.

1.2   Feature Movement

In his first paper developing the Minimalist Program, Chomsky (1993) suggested that covert phrasal movement is the default style of movement. He implemented this idea by means of a principle called *Procrastinate*, which required movement to be covert. This principle, in turn, was argued to be overruled whenever movement is motivated by a "strong" feature. In this system a strong feature was a feature that needed to be "checked" by overt movement, in order to avoid violating the principle of Full Interpretation at PF. Though this proposal provoked much interesting research and discussion, it had a certain arbitrariness about it, in that it was not obvious (at least at the conceptual level) why language should incorporate a timing principle like Procrastinate. Why not the opposite timing principle (e.g., the Earliness Principle developed in Pesetsky 1989, as incorporated, for example, in Brody's (1995) "radically minimalist" model), or no timing principle at all?

In later work Chomsky (1995) offered an alternative view that promised to eliminate the issue. He suggested that it had been a mistake to assume that covert movement is ever "phrasal." Chomsky's (1995) proposal starts with the idea that movement is a "repair strategy" by which an uninterpretable feature F on a head K is deleted in response to movement to K of another instance of F (typically an interpretable instance of F). Failure to repair a structure that contains an uninterpretable feature renders the derivation nonconvergent. Movement for any other purpose is banned. For example, an uninterpretable *wh*-feature on C might require movement of the corresponding *wh*-feature from a *wh*-phrase elsewhere in the structure, but there could be no "gratuitous" movement of this feature in other circumstances. Likewise, an uninterpretable person feature on T requires movement of a person feature from some DP internal to the structure containing T (gratuitous instances of this movement strategy being prohibited). On this view movement at its simplest should copy just the features necessary to ensure convergence (Chomsky 1995, 262). Copying of anything more than features is unexpected—especially the phonological features and dependent constituents copied in overt phrasal movement.

In this system phrasal movement is, in a sense, the surprise. Phrasal movement arises when a grammatical feature that must be moved cannot be separated from the syntactic expression in which it occurs. In the case of overt DP-movement to subject position ([Spec, TP]), for example, it is supposed that the D-feature cannot be copied apart from the remainder of the expression that it labels. Likewise, overt *wh*-phrase movement is attributed to the inability of the phonological system to pronounce the *wh*-feature and the remainder of its phrase in separate places. Chomsky suggests that when a feature moves, "[it] carries along just enough material for convergence" (1995, 262). Movement of more than just the relevant feature occurs only if "generalized pied-piping" is necessary for the derivation to converge at LF or PF. Chomsky further speculates that only PF considerations force pied-piping of this sort.[8]

Chomsky's (1995) proposal leaves us with two types of movement. Movement that copies a phrase is motivated by PF considerations and must by its very nature be "overt" movement. Movement that copies only the grammatical features that motivate the movement must be "covert" movement. On this view, then, feature movement is simply the proper

analysis of covert movement—"covert" in the sense that it has no effect
on the phonology, and postulation of covert *phrasal* movement was
simply an error. Notice that this view, if correct, offers a third slant on
the overt/covert contrast—distinct from both the Y-model and single-
output syntax traditions. The proposal that covert movement is feature
movement removes any need for either syntactic timing or phonological
principles to distinguish the two movement types.[9] Covert and overt
movement may take place in a single syntactic cycle, phonological distinctions arising simply from differences in the material copied by the
movement operation. Chomsky (1995) did not develop this consequence
of his new view of movement, but it follows straightforwardly, nonetheless. In Chomsky 1998 he takes exactly this step.

Chomsky's (1995) proposal concerning movement is consonant with
some arguments for covert movement, but not all. It is, of course, consonant with any test that cares only about the relation between a source and
a target—for example, the command condition discussed in connection
with (8). However, it runs afoul of evidence for covert movement that
identifies the moving element as a word or phrase. As we saw, evidence
from ACD has just this property. ACD resolution *requires* movement of
an entire phrase out of categories that contain it (a conclusion supported
by Fiengo and May's (1994) binding theory evidence, as explained by Fox
(1995)[10]).

Consequently, it does not appear correct to simply reanalyze covert
phrasal movement as feature movement. Covert phrasal movement exists.
I suspect that this conclusion is not a step backward. Although Chomsky's (1995) proposal provides a rationale for his earlier assumption that
covert movement is the default type of movement, it is not clear that the
earlier assumption was correct. I know of no empirical evidence bearing
on the matter, nor is it obvious how the conceptual chips fall. Indeed,
alongside the plausible-sounding idea that the most natural style of movement would copy just the features needed to ensure convergence, one
might lay a quite different, equally plausible idea: that movement copies
the *largest constituent* that bears the relevant feature. This idea would
make phrasal movement (rather than feature movement) the default.
Each of these ideas is natural. Let us view movement as a process by
which a head H in search of a feature F scans down the tree in order to
identify a constituent that bears F and copies it. According to Chomsky's
(1995) idea, only the feature is copied; according to the alternative, the

identified constituent is copied. I am hard pressed to find even an Occam's razor argument that favors one idea over the other.[11]

On the other hand, whatever one's views of the actual proposals, one can distill an important question from the discussion. Granted that movement, both overt and covert, does sometimes copy phrases, are there movement operations that simply establish a relationship between expressions bearing a particular *feature*? I will suggest that the answer is yes. If so, then Chomsky's (1995) discussion of feature movement uncovered something real—but misidentified the discovery. The phenomenon that Chomsky called "feature movement" is not an alternative analysis of covert phrasal movement, as he thought, but a distinct syntactic operation in its own right.[12]

To see in a nutshell what I have in mind, compare the behavior of *wh*-in-situ with the behavior of the "associate" in the English existential *there* construction. As is well known, the verb in the English existential *there*-construction generally agrees with a postverbal "associate" DP, which is usually required to be indefinite.

Agreement with the associate DP in the there *construction*
(16) a. There is a book on the table.
    b. There are some books on the table.

(17) a. There is likely to be a book on the table.
    b. There are likely to be some books on the table.

Apparently, Merge of *there* as a specifier of TP satisfies the "Extended Projection Principle" requirements of T (its need for a phrasal specifier), but does not satisfy the requirement that T "check" (i.e., delete) its number features (and possibly others). The word *there*, Chomsky suggests (1995, 273), does not bear these features. Consequently, the features must move to T from somewhere inside TP. The associate DP furnishes the necessary features.

Feature movement from the associate DP in the there *construction*
(18) a. There [F_i-is] [F_i-a book] on the table.
    b. There [F_i-are] [F_i-some books] on the table.

(19) a. There [F_i-is] likely to be [F_i-a book] on the table.
    b. There [F_i-are] likely to be [F_i-some books] on the table.

There is thus a movement-like relation between the associate and T. This relation is "covert," in that neither the associate nor T seems to show any phonological effect of the relationship (besides the agreement relation itself). Nonetheless, the relation is real. For one thing, c-command must be maintained between T and the associate.

C-command condition on feature movement
(20) a.   He said there [F$_i$-were] likely to be [F$_i$-several books] on the
          table.
     b. *... and likely to be [F$_i$-several books] on the table there are.

Furthermore, the associate must be the closest DP to T.

Ban on superraising with overt phrasal movement
(21) *Several books$_i$ are desirable [for it to be t$_i$ on the table].

The relation between the associate and T in the *there* construction is blocked in exactly the same circumstances.

Ban on superraising with feature movement
(22) *There are desirable for it to be several semanticists at the party.

   So far the relation between the associate and T is revealed by evidence familiar from arguments for covert movement (movement without a phonological effect). But is the relation covert *phrasal* movement of the associate to T? ACD provides a means of detecting phrasal movement and strongly suggests that the answer is no.

   To see this, we must attach a relative clause containing VP-ellipsis to an associate of *there* and test for the possibility of using a higher VP as an antecedent for the elided VP. For reasons that are unclear to me, a relative clause attached to an associate in the *there* construction favors an associate containing a strong quantifier like *every*, rather than the typical indefinite—but some weak associates like *no one* are also natural.

Relative clauses compatible with an associate
(23) a.   There will be [everyone that there should [$_{VP}$ be t]] at the party.
     b.   There will be [almost no one that there should [$_{VP}$ be t]] at the
          party.

Next we should ensure that VP-ellipsis is compatible in principle with the *there* construction. Example (24) shows that it is.

VP-ellipsis acceptable in the there-*associate construction*
(24) Will there be phonologists at the party? Well, there should [$_{VP}$ Δ].

If we now elide the VP in (23), we have our test for ACD. The examples in (25) display the crucial contrast with (23).

ACD impossible in a relative clause modifying an associate[13]
(25) a. *There will be [everyone that there should [$_{VP}$ Δ]] at the party.
    b. *There will be [almost no one that there should [$_{VP}$ Δ]] at the party.

Since (24) shows that there is nothing wrong with the ellipsis per se, the unacceptability of ACD in (25) shows that—whatever is transpiring between the associate and T in a *there* construction—it is not phrasal movement.[14] Instead, it appears to be movement of something (obligatorily) smaller than the associate phrase. Feature movement fits the bill.[15] This conclusion accords with Chomsky's (1995, 272ff.) hypothesis that long-distance agreement in the *there* construction is a consequence of feature movement.

In the case of the *there* construction, the feature movement hypothesis revises an earlier set of proposals, also by Chomsky (1986b), in which the movement properties of the associate-T relation were attributed to covert phrasal movement. Though Chomsky did not base an argument for this revision on ACD, it does provide a strong argument in its favor. If we accept this conclusion, however, we need an explanation for the contrast between the "associate-in-situ" in the *there* construction and *wh*-in-situ in multiple questions. In each case we find evidence of a relation between a phrase pronounced in situ and a higher position. But the two constructions behave differently under a test for specifically *phrasal* covert movement. Whereas covert movement of the associate in the *there* construction looks like feature movement, covert movement of *wh*-in-situ looks like phrasal movement. It is this pattern of evidence that suggests the existence of more than one type of movement-like relationship between syntactic positions.

I will take these conclusions as my point of departure, devoting considerable attention to distinctions between phrasal movement and "feature movement" in Chomsky's (1995) sense. Later, however, I will also examine some possible variants of this picture—though I will leave the choice among alternatives open. In particular, I will entertain the possibility that "feature movement" is actually a subcomponent of phrasal movement. I will attribute the similarities between the two operations to that fact, rather than to the existence of two substantially different varieties of movement. Note, for example, that there is no clear evidence that features of the associate in the *there* construction actually "move" to a position near T. Instead, the evidence points to some sort of communication between the features of the associate and the features of T. For now, however, I will stick to more familiar concepts like "movement" and will present my arguments as evidence for the coexistence of phrasal and feature movement in grammar.

I am now in a position to sketch the goals of the book in some detail. If the discussion so far is on the right track, we might expect to find "minimal triplets" in which a particular head establishes a relationship with a remote feature in each of the three ways we have seen—the choice depending on other properties of the grammar. That is, we might expect to find movement to a particular head showing up sometimes as overt phrasal movement, sometimes as covert phrasal movement, and sometimes as feature movement. The existence of such a "minimal triplet" is not logically entailed by my hypotheses. Nonetheless, if we can identify such a triplet, we will significantly improve our ability to investigate the coexistence of phrasal movement with feature movement in the grammar, since we will have the opportunity to examine the differences among these syntactic operations under well-controlled conditions.

In the remainder of this book I present and investigate a triplet of exactly this sort. In particular, I will argue that interrogative *wh*-constructions involve relations of all three types. We have already seen examples of overt and covert phrasal *wh*-movement to C in English. I will suggest that under certain circumstances we can detect another kind of operation that relates *wh*-phrases to an interrogative C: feature movement (or something very much like it).

I introduced Bulgarian into the discussion of English multiple questions with malice aforethought, since Bulgarian provides some of the foundations of the argument I will present. After giving evidence in favor of covert phrasal movement for *wh*-in-situ, I noted (in the footsteps of Lasnik and Saito (1984)) that on this view Bulgarian simply shows overt phrasal movement where English shows its covert counterpart (see the summary of this difference in (14)–(15)). In the next chapter I present certain other facts about Bulgarian multiple questions and offer partial explanations (borrowed from Richards 1997). In chapters 2–4 I show that a seemingly distinct set of puzzles concerning English multiple questions actually represents the same phenomena observed in Bulgarian. If this is true, I can claim that the pronunciation distinctions in (14) and (15) constitute the *only* relevant difference between multiple questions in the two languages. However, I only reach this conclusion if I assume that in certain cases multiple questions in English (and Bulgarian) involve pure feature movement of *wh*—even though in other cases they involve overt and covert phrasal movement triggered by the same feature. In chapter 5 I consider syntactic and semantic consequences of this hypothesis, a discussion that helps establish a crosslinguistic typology of *wh*-movement.

1.3   Superiority Effects

The English puzzles involve the observation known as the *Superiority effect*. The Superiority effect arises in a multiple question when more than one *wh*-phrase is relevant to the answering patterns for the question. In such a case the syntax needs to decide on a pattern of *wh*-movement within that question. The Superiority effect is a restriction on this decision. In English, where only one *wh*-phrase moves overtly, the Superiority effect is responsible for the contrast observed in (26)–(27).

Superiority effect
(26) a.   Who ____ bought what?
      b.   *What did who buy ____?

(27) a.   Who did you persuade ____ to read what?
      b.   ??What did you persuade whom to read ____?

If we assume that the first application of *wh*-movement in these examples is the overt phrasal instance of *wh*-movement, Kuno and Robinson's (1972) description of the phenomenon is accurate.

Kuno and Robinson's constraint
(28) A *wh*-word cannot be preposed crossing over another *wh*.

Chomsky (1973) suggested that (28) is a special case of a more general phenomenon, which he termed the *Superiority Condition*.

Superiority Condition
(29) No rule can involve X, Y in the structure
      . . . X . . . [$_\alpha$ . . . Z . . .–WYV . . .]
      where the rule applies ambiguously to Z and Y and Z is superior to [m-commands] Y.

Chomsky's later condition (1995, 280, 296), which I will call *Attract Closest* (AC), is in essence a restatement of the Superiority Condition for movement, where movement is viewed as triggered by particular features of a "target" head K.

Attract Closest
(30) α can raise to target K only if there is no legitimate operation
      Move β targeting K, where β is closer to K.

When one presents the examples in (26)–(27) to speakers in a manner that is fair to the data (maintaining focal stress on *wh*-in-situ in both cases, and presenting the examples without special context), the contrasts are clear and stable. Nonetheless, there are minimal changes that one can make in these examples that produce apparent exceptions to the Superiority effect. These facts will be crucial to the investigation.

1.3.1   D-Linking

One minimal change of this sort involves what I have elsewhere (Pesetsky 1987) called *D-linking*. When a *wh*-question asks for answers in which the individuals that replace the *wh*-phrases are drawn from a set that is presumed to be salient to both speaker and hearer, the multiple question can appear to violate AC. This possibility typically arises when the answers to the question are supposed to be drawn from a set of individuals previously introduced into the discourse, or when the set forms part of the "common ground" shared by speaker and hearer. *Wh*-phrases with *which* favor this type of interpretation.

Superiority effect disappears with D-linking

(31) a. Which person ____ bought which book?
     b. Which book did which person buy ____?

(32) a. Which person did John talk to ____ about which topic?
     b. Which topic did John talk to which person about ____?

The semantics of D-linked *wh*-phrases closely tracks the semantics of the definite article *the*. Context sets previously mentioned in the discourse qualify a phrase as D-linked, but so do sets that are merely salient (e.g., *which book*, in a context where speaker and hearer both know that reference is being made to a reading list for a course) and sets whose salience is culturally determined (e.g., *what day of the week*, *which sign of the zodiac*). A reliable rule of thumb is that if a *wh*-word in a multiple question can be felicitously paraphrased with an expression of the form *which of the X*, it can cause the Superiority effect to disappear. The reason for this link between semantics and syntax is obscure, and will remain obscure even at the end of this book. On the other hand, the syntax of the problem is also obscure: What is the structure of D-linked questions in which the Superiority effect appears to be obviated?[16] Are they exceptions to AC, or is something else going on? By the end of the book I hope to have answered *these* questions quite fully.

1.3.2   More than Two *Wh*-Phrases

The next factor is less studied, but equally striking.[17] The Superiority effect is limited to questions with two *wh*-phrases. It disappears in multiple questions with more than two *wh*-phrases.[18]

Superiority effect disappears with more than two wh-*phrases*

(33) a. *What did who give ____ to Mary?   [detectable Superiority effect]

     b. What did who give ____ to whom?   [no detectable Superiority effect]

I will discuss this effect in greater detail later. For now I simply wish to note the important syntactic questions this contrast raises. They are the same as the ones posed previously: What is the structure of questions with more than two *wh*-phrases, in which the Superiority effect appears to be obviated? Are they exceptions to AC, or is something else going on?

1.3.3   German

Another minimal change in a multiple question that obviates the Superiority effect is translation into German. In at least the simplest cases, German appears to lack the Superiority contrast entirely.

Superiority effect disappears in German

(34) a. Ich weiß nicht, wer was gesehen hat.
        I   know not   who what seen   has
        'I don't know who has seen what.'

     b. Ich weiß nicht, was wer gesehen hat.
        I   know not   what who seen   has
        'I don't know what who has seen.'

The correct interpretation of this fact is a matter of controversy, which I will turn to in sections 5.3 and 5.4. For now it is sufficient to observe the problem and to ask the same questions posed about the previous two sets of apparent counterexamples.

These are the problems that will occupy the remainder of this book. In the next chapter I present a fuller picture of Bulgarian multiple questions, as necessary background to the discussion of apparent exceptions to the Superiority effect.

Chapter 2

Two Observations about Bulgarian

2.1 A Complementizer That Requires Multiple Specifiers

I have already noted that Bulgarian (unlike English) shows multiple instances of overt phrasal *wh*-movement to the left periphery of CP. So far I have said nothing about the obligatoriness or optionality of multiple overt movement. The obligatoriness of multiple overt movement partly depends on D-linking, in ways I discuss later. For now I consider only multiple questions without a D-linked interpretation. In these cases the facts are somewhat subtle.

Consider a question containing three *wh*-phrases. According to consultants' judgments, in the most natural multiple question using three *wh*-phrases, all three are overtly fronted, as in (35a). Nonetheless, a construction in which only two of the *wh*-phrases are fronted is fairly acceptable. By contrast, a multiple question in which only one *wh*-phrase is overtly fronted is strongly unacceptable (in the non-D-linked usage being considered). There is thus a three-way contrast. The diacritics ("**" vs. "??" vs. "OK") are those supplied by one of my consultants, Roumyana Izvorski, but the general description of the judgments contrasts perfection with unnaturalness with total unacceptability: the break between (35b–c) and (35d) is claimed to be sharper than that between (35a) and (35b–c).[19] ((35a–d) were supplied by Roumyana Izvorski and Ivan Derzhanski.)

Fronting different numbers of wh-*phrases (Bulgarian)*
(35) a.　Koj kakvo na kogo　dade?　[all *wh*-phrases move]
　　　　who what　to whom gave
　　　　'Who gave what to whom?'
　　 b.　??Koj na kogo dade kakvo?　[2 *wh*-phrases move]

    c. ??Koj kakvo dade na kogo?   [2 *wh*-phrases move]
    d. **Koj dade kakvo na kogo?   [only 1 *wh*-phrase moves]

Since there seems to be no reason to assume that the Bulgarian *wh*-phrases in a multiple question are related to distinct heads (Rudin 1988), we may safely assume that these phrases all bear the specifier relation to the same interrogative head, in the manner posited by Koizumi (1995) and Ura (1996). I will call this interrogative head the *multispecifier complementizer* ($C_{m\text{-}spec}$), to indicate that its "specifier potential" requires it to take more than one specifier. The ability of $C_{m\text{-}spec}$ to attract more than one *wh*-phrase indicates that the feature of $C_{m\text{-}spec}$ responsible for *wh*-movement (uninterpretable though it may be) does not need to delete and does not exhaust its ability to motivate *wh*-movement until its maximal projection has been fully built. It is thus possible to propose that (36) is true and that (36) and (37) are jointly responsible for the three-way split in judgments on Bulgarian multiple questions.[20]

Specifier potential of $C_{m\text{-}spec}$
(36) $C_{m\text{-}spec}$ requires more than one *wh*-specifier.

General preference
(37) All *wh*-phrases in a multiple question move.

I will assume that $C_{m\text{-}spec}$ differs both syntactically and semantically from the standard interrogative complementizer $C_{1\text{-}spec}$, which takes a single *wh*-specifier.

Specifier potential of $C_{1\text{-}spec}$
(38) $C_{1\text{-}spec}$ requires one *wh*-specifier.

A multiple question in English or Bulgarian *must* be introduced by $C_{m\text{-}spec}$ (and a nonmultiple question must be introduced by $C_{1\text{-}spec}$). Consequently, (35d) cannot slip through the net of constraints discussed in this section by using the complementizer reserved for nonmultiple questions. (I discuss the typology of complementizers in more detail in chapter 5).[21]

Besides the multiple-specifier requirement of $C_{m\text{-}spec}$, there must be another condition with the effect of requiring at least one instance of phrasal *wh*-movement in an embedded question, so as to rule out (39a) with *wh*-feature movement from *what*. The specifier properties of $C_{1\text{-}spec}$ ensure the contrast in (39) and its Bulgarian counterparts. The pronunciation principles guarantee that the one specifier required by $C_{1\text{-}spec}$ will be overt.

C$_{1\text{-spec}}$ in English
(39) a. *Mary needs to know [Bill saw what].
    b. Mary needs to know [what Bill saw].

An alternative view of the Bulgarian data deserves attention. On this view the only factor influencing judgments is (37), sentences being judged gradiently according to how many *wh*-phrases violate it. To decide between these two proposals on the basis of Bulgarian data, we must examine the behavior of questions with four (or more) *wh*-phrases. The two statements in (36)–(37) predict a three-way contrast in such a case. Moving all four *wh*-phrases would be perfect; moving two or three of the four *wh*-phrases would be indistinguishably unnatural to a mild degree; and moving only one *wh*-phrase would be unacceptable. To the extent that such a paradigm can be constructed without running afoul of other complications, the facts seem to support (36)–(37). For example, in (40) a ditransitive verb and an instrumental phrase furnish the four *wh*-phrases. According to the judgments of Roumyana Izvorski (personal communication), there is a major acceptability break between (40a–c) and (40d).[22]

Four wh-*phrases: monoclausal examples*
(40) a.   Koj na kogo kakvo s   kakvo napisa?   [all *wh*-phrases move]
         who to whom what with what wrote
         'Who wrote what to whom with what?'
    b.   ?Koj na kogo kakvo napisa s kakvo?   [3 out of 4 *wh*-phrases move]
    c.   ???Koj na kogo napisa kakvo s kakvo?   [2 out of 4 *wh*-phrases move]
    d.   **Koj napisa kakvo na kogo s kakvo?   [1 out of 4 *wh*-phrases moves]

Similar tests can be performed with biclausal structures. Once again there is a major acceptability break, between (41a–c) and (41d).

Four wh-*phrases: biclausal examples*
(41) a.   Koj kogo na kogo kakvo ubedi   da dade?
         who whom to whom what convinced to give
         'Who convinced whom to give what to whom?'
    b.   ?Koj kogo na kogo ubedi da dade kakvo?
    c.   ???Koj kogo ubedi na kogo da dade kakvo?
    d.   **Koj ubedi kogo da dade kakvo na kogo?

2.2   Superiority Effects and the Principle of Minimal Compliance

So far I have not considered how *wh*-phrases in a Bulgarian multiple question are ordered.[23] As Rudin (1988) observes, the order of *wh*-phrases in a Bulgarian multiple question conforms to the generalization in (42), exemplified in (43)–(44). In other words, the contrast between Bulgarian (43a) and (43b) corresponds to an English Superiority effect.[24]

Superiority effect (Bulgarian)

(42) The leftmost *wh*-phrase in a Bulgarian multiple question is the *wh*-phrase that moves overtly in the corresponding English multiple question.

(43) a.   Koj kakvo vižda?
           who what   sees
           [cf. *Who sees what?*]
     b. *Kakvo koj vižda?
           [cf. **What does who see?*]

(44) a.   Koj kŭde   udari Ivan?
           who where hit   Ivan
           [cf. *Who hit Ivan where?*]
     b. *Kŭde koj udari Ivan?
           [cf. **Where did who hit Ivan?*]

The Superiority effect in English follows naturally from Attract Closest (AC), on the assumption that the overt instance of phrasal *wh*-movement in English is also the first instance of phrasal *wh*-movement in the derivation. By parity of reasoning, the leftmost *wh*-phrase in a Bulgarian question is also the first to move. This means that the second *wh*-phrase must have "tucked in" underneath the first phrase, forming a lower specifier than the *wh*-phrase that moved first.

"Tucking in"

(45) a.   Koj kŭde C ____ udari Ivan ____?

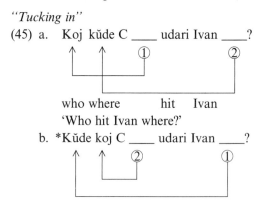

           who where   hit   Ivan
           'Who hit Ivan where?'
     b. *Kŭde koj C ____ udari Ivan ____?

This is, in fact, the hypothesis advanced by Richards (1997), who conducted an extensive study of multiple-attraction constructions in Bulgarian and other languages. As Richards points out, second instances of movement to a given attractor *should* "tuck in" if, in addition to the "attractor-oriented" condition AC, movement also obeys a "mover-oriented" condition, *Shortest Move*. The first *wh*-phrase to be attracted by C in (44a) is, because of AC, the highest C in the structure. (I will assign the label wh_1 to the *wh*-phrase of a question that occupies the highest structural position *before wh*-movement, and similarly for other *wh*-phrases.) Wh_1 moves as short a distance as possible, which in this case creates the first specifier of C. The second *wh* to be attracted in constructions like those in (43)–(44) is the other *wh*-phrase: wh_2. This *wh*-phrase could in principle create a specifier higher than wh_1, or it could create a specifier lower than wh_1. Shortest Move favors creation of a specifier lower than wh_1—that is, "tucking in" as in (45a). In this way, the interaction of AC and Shortest Move causes the command relations between two *wh*-phrases after movement to mirror their order before movement.[25]

As Richards notes, a tucking-in derivation is "countercyclic" in that it does not extend the tree. This would violate the Strict Cycle Condition if each category were to count as a cycle—as suggested by Chomsky (1993) under the rubric of the Extension Condition, which requires each overt operation to extend the tree at its root. Richards suggests that it is not the tucking-in hypothesis but the Extension Condition that is incorrect. The cases that actually motivated the Extension Condition and its predecessors involve derivations in which the overt-movement requirements of a lower head are satisfied later than the overt-movement requirements of a higher head. In later work Chomsky (1995) suggests an alternative approach that zeros in more tightly on the actual cases that need to be excluded. He suggests that convergent derivations must satisfy the overt-movement requirements of a head H while still building the portion of the tree headed by H. (In his terminology, failure to satisfy the "strong feature" of a head H in a timely fashion "cancels the derivation.") This proposal, which Richards calls *featural cyclicity*, blocks most traditional Strict Cycle Condition violations, but allows tucking in as in (45a), precisely because tucking in involves countercyclic movements to a single head.[26]

Now let us consider AC more closely—in particular, its effects in multiple questions with three or more *wh*-phrases. All things being equal, one might expect AC to be obeyed in some fashion in each instance of *wh*-attraction to $C_{m\text{-spec}}$. For example, in a multiple question with three overtly moved *wh*-phrases, one might expect their order after movement to mirror their order before movement—just as in a multiple question with two overtly moved *wh*-phrases. As Bošković (1995, 1998) notes, however, this is not the case. Though the leftmost *wh* after movement must be the highest *wh* before movement, the second *wh* after movement is *not* required to be the second highest *wh* before movement. The orders $wh_1\ wh_2\ wh_3$ and $wh_1\ wh_3\ wh_2$ are equal (or nearly equal) in acceptability.

Wh$_1$ wh$_2$ wh$_3$ and wh$_1$ wh$_3$ wh$_2$ both acceptable
(46) a. Koj na kogo   kakvo dade?
          who to whom what   gave
          'Who gave what to whom?'
      b. ?Koj kakvo na kogo dade?

(47) a. Koj kogo   kak udari?
          who whom how hit
          'Who hit whom how?'
      b. Koj kak kogo udari?

(48) a. Koj kogo   kakvo e   pital?
          who whom what   AUX asked
          'Who asked whom what?'
      b. Koj kakvo kogo e pital?

   The AC requirement seems to be "turned off" for movement to a given $C_{\text{m-spec}}$ once it has been satisfied by a prior operation of *wh*-movement to that $C_{\text{m-spec}}$. As Richards puts it, it is as if the first operation of *wh*-movement pays an "AC tax" that allows subsequent instances of *wh*-movement to the same target to ignore this constraint, as in the following sketch of a derivation for (46b):

Paying the "AC tax"
(49) a. *Before* wh-*movement*
          $C_{\text{m-spec}}$ [koj dade na kogo kakvo]
      b. *Step 1*
          $C_{\text{m-spec}}$ attracts the *wh*-feature of *koj* (wh_1), pays "AC tax."
          koj C [____ dade na kogo kakvo]
      c. *Step 2*
          $C_{\text{m-spec}}$ attracts either of the remaining *wh*-phrases, since "AC tax" has been paid. *Wh*-phrase tucks in under *koj*.
          koj kakvo C [____ dade na kogo ____]
      d. *Step 3*
          $C_{\text{m-spec}}$ attracts the other *wh*-phrase, which tucks in under *kakvo*.
          koj kakvo na kogo C [____ dade ____ ____]

Richards (1997) argues that this view of the matter is exactly correct. He suggests further that the logic of the "AC tax" is a special case of a much more general metaconstraint that he calls the *Principle of Minimal Compliance* (PMC). The precise characterization of this more general principle (see Richards 1997) is not important here. The relevant phenomenon is the simple observation that "attractor-oriented" constraints on movement apply only to the first movement operation that targets a given attractor.

Principle of Minimal Compliance
(50) For any dependency D that obeys constraint C, any elements that are relevant for determining whether D obeys C can be ignored for the rest of the derivation for purposes of determining whether any other dependency D' obeys C.

An element X is *relevant* to determining whether a dependency D with head A and tail B obeys constraint C iff
a. X is along the path of D (that is, X = A, X = B, or A c-commands X and X c-commands B), and
b. X is a member of the class of elements to which C makes reference.

PMC for our purposes
(51) Once an instance of movement to α has obeyed a constraint on the distance between source and target, other instances of movement to α need not obey this constraint.

The PMC applies to a number of syntactic conditions. Certain island effects, such as Ross's (1967) Complex NP Constraint, hold in their strongest form only of the first instance of *wh*-movement to a given C. The Bulgarian example (52a), for instance, displays the expected judgment for *wh*-movement out of a clause contained inside an NP. Example (52b) contains exactly the same instance of *wh*-movement as (52a), except that here it is (by hypothesis) the second instance of movement to its target, rather than the first. Strikingly, the effects on acceptability of the Complex NP Constraint violation fade nearly to the vanishing point.[27] (Data from Roumyana Izvorski, Ani Petkova, and Roumyana Slabakova, in personal communication to Norvin Richards; see Richards 1997.)

PMC improves Subjacency violations
(52) a. *Koja kniga otreče senatorăt [mălvata   če   iska   da zabrani ____]?
          which book denied the-senator the-rumor that wanted to ban
          'Which book did the senator deny the rumor that he wanted to ban?'

b. ?Koj   senator koja   kniga otreče ____ [mălvata   če   iska   da zabrani ____]?

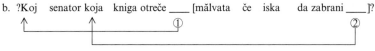

which senator which book denied   the-rumor that wanted to ban
'Which senator denied the rumor that he wanted to ban which book?'

These facts recall properties of English multiple questions. As is well known, *wh*-in-situ in English multiple questions do not display island effects—or at least display them very weakly (Hankamer 1974). This fact has always been a puzzle, particularly if, as I have argued, *wh*-in-situ standardly undergo covert *wh*-movement. Traditional accounts (e.g., Huang 1982) attribute the absence of island effects in these environments to a special fact about covert *wh*-movement. As Richards notes, the phenomenon can instead be seen as the English counterpart of the effect in (52). On this view, Subjacency effects are absent with covert *wh*-movement in multiple questions not because the movement is covert, but because it follows an earlier application of *wh*-movement in its clause.[28]

In this respect Richards's Bulgarian discoveries perfectly mirror data from Italian discovered by Longobardi (1991), as analyzed by Brody (1995). Bulgarian exhibits multiple instances of overt movement, the first instance paying the "Subjacency tax" that allows later instances to bypass the Subjacency effect. Italian exhibits multiple instances of *covert* movement with the same properties. The Italian case does not involve *wh*-movement, but scope assignment to negative phrases. I follow Brody's presentation here. A negative phrase like *nessuno* 'no one' and its scope position (marked by *non* with postverbal negation) can be separated by embedded clauses.

Long-distance scope (Italian)
(53) Non approverei   che tu gli consentissi di vedere nessuno.
     NEG I-would-approve that you him allow   to see   no-one
     'I would not approve that you allow him to see anybody.'

Nonetheless, the relationship obeys adjunct islands (as shown in (54a)) and subject islands (as shown in (54b)). This fact leads one to suspect that covert movement of the negative element takes place.

Long-distance scope obeys islands (Italian)
(54) a. * Non fa   il suo dovere per aiutare nessuno.
          NEG does his   duty   for to-help no-one
          'He does not do his duty in order to help anyone.'

b. ?*Chiamare nessuno sarà   possibile.
to-call   no-one   will-be possible
'It will not be possible to call anyone.'

Crucially, when two negative phrases share the same scope, the lower phrase does not have to obey the islands seen in (54).

PMC improves island violations (Italian)
(55) a. ?Chiamare nessuno servirà   a   niente, ormai.
to-call   no-one   will-serve for nothing now
'To call no one will do any good now.'
b. Non fa   niente   per aiutare nessuno.
NEG does nothing for to-help no-one
'He does not do anything in order to help anyone.'

English, Bulgarian, and Italian thus all display the same phenomenon: the first occurrence of movement to a given position obeys islands, but the second does not—whether the two movements differ in overtness (English), are both overt (Bulgarian), or are both covert (Italian).[29]

A cautionary note is in order. Although AC is subject to the PMC, Shortest Move is another matter. Once a given instance of movement to a given C has satisfied Shortest Move, it must not be the case that subsequent instances of movement to that C may violate Shortest Move; if they did, we could not observe a "tucking in" requirement. This follows if Shortest Move is not a constraint governing the distance between an attractor and an attractee, but a constraint that chooses the exact position near a given attractor to which copying takes place.

2.3 Summary of Bulgarian *Wh*-Movement

I have made the following observations about Bulgarian:

• *Multiple-specifier requirement:* The complementizer of a multiple question in Bulgarian appears to strongly require at least two *wh*-phrases as specifiers. This is a separate requirement from the general preference for moving all *wh*-phrases in a multiple question.
• *Superiority:* The leftmost *wh*-phrase in a multiple question is the *wh*-phrase that was highest before movement—wh_1 in the terminology used here. If this is the same fact as the Superiority effect in English, it suggests that the leftmost *wh*-phrase is also the first to move. This entails that multiple movement to a given head proceeds via "tucking in."

• *The PMC:* In Bulgarian, AC is only required to be satisfied by the first instance of phrasal *wh*-movement to C. Consequently, the second *wh*-phrase to move is not necessarily the second highest *wh*-phrase before movement (wh_2).

Finally, it is now apparent that the pronunciation principles in (14)–(15), repeated here, were appropriately formulated—assuming, of course, that it was correct to identify the leftmost *wh*-phrase in Bulgarian with the single overtly moved *wh*-phrase in English.

Pronunciation rule (English)

(56) a. The first instance of *wh*-phrase movement to C is *overt*, in that *wh* is pronounced in its new position and unpronounced in its trace positions.

 b. Secondary instances of *wh*-phrase movement to C are *covert*, in that *wh* is pronounced in its trace position and unpronounced in its new position.

Pronunciation rule (Bulgarian)

(57) All *wh*-phrase movement to C is *overt*, in that *wh* is pronounced in its new position and unpronounced in its trace positions.

As promised earlier, I will argue that (56) and (57) are the *only* relevant differences between English and Bulgarian *wh*-questions. In particular, once *wh*-feature movement is introduced into the discussion, we will see that several peculiarities of English multiple questions are simply the reflection, in English, of the Bulgarian properties summarized in this section.[30] Having discussed phrasal movement versus feature movement in chapter 1 and sketched Bulgarian *wh*-syntax in this chapter, I can now develop the argument.

Chapter 3

Does Wh_1-in-Situ Undergo Covert Phrasal Movement?

3.1 No

As noted earlier, *wh*-questions show apparent exceptions to Attract Closest (AC), over and above those attributable to the Principle of Minimal Compliance (PMC). These are cases in which wh_1 is pronounced in situ, while some other *wh*-phrase is pronounced in [Spec, CP]. (I describe the situation in terms of pronunciation only so as not to prejudge the actual movement patterns.) One exception of this type mentioned in chapter 1 involves D-linking. Relevant examples were given in (31)–(32), of which (31) is repeated here.

D-linking apparent exception to Superiority
(58) a. Which person ____ bought which book?
     b. Which book did which person buy ____?

Example (58a) shows wh_1 (presumably) moved and pronounced in [Spec, CP].[31] Example (58b), on the other hand, shows wh_2 moved and wh_1 in situ. Obviously, the acceptability of (58b) reveals an inadequacy somewhere in the previous discussion—but where? To answer this question, we need to know what the syntax of (58b) is.

• For example, does wh_1, the in-situ *wh*-phrase in (58b), undergo phrasal *wh*-movement of some sort? If the in-situ *wh*-phrase *does* undergo phrasal movement, the movement is obviously covert. If so, we must ask why. Did wh_1, the higher *wh*-phrase, undergo phrasal movement first—but the output of movement was pronounced as covert movement for some reason, in violation of the pronunciation rule (56)? Or was AC violated, so that the first *wh* attracted was wh_2, the lower *wh* (with the pronunciation rule (56) operating exactly as expected)?

• If, however, the in-situ *wh*-phrase does *not* undergo phrasal movement, we must also ask why. Is wh_1 in (58b) for some reason ineligible for *wh*-movement? Or is AC violable in situations other than those given by the PMC? Or is something else going on?

Clearly, the first issue to settle is whether or not wh_1 undergoes phrasal movement. We have in our repertoire exactly one test for specifically phrasal movement: antecedent-contained deletion (ACD). We have already used this test as part of an argument that *wh*-in-situ may in principle undergo covert phrasal movement. The relevant cases were examples like (12a–b), repeated here, in which a relative clause modifying a *wh*-phrase in situ contains an instance of ACD.

Wh-*in-situ licenses ACD*
(59) a. Which girl invited [which student that John did [$_{VP}$ Δ]]?
   b. I need to know who can speak [which languages that Ken Hale can [$_{VP}$ Δ]].

These examples, of course, do not involve any apparent exception to the Superiority effect. Neither example shows wh_1-in-situ, so neither example tests whether the covert phrasal movement detected in (59) is also available to wh_1-in-situ. By attaching a modifier that contains ACD to an otherwise legal instance of wh_1-in-situ, we should be able to determine (all things being equal) whether this type of *wh*-in-situ also undergoes covert phrasal movement. Although the relevant examples are (inevitably) complex, the experiment is straightforward and its results are clear.

Let us begin by constructing, as an experimental control, a slightly more complex counterpart to the examples in (59), containing three relevant DP positions. Example (60a) is the necessary control. The three DP positions that we will work with are the subject of *order*, the object of *order*, and the object of *congratulate*. I have glossed (60a) with its intended interpretation, (60b).

Wh$_1$ *not in situ, ACD within* wh$_2$
(60) a. I need to know which girl ____ ordered [which boy that Mary (also) did Δ] to congratulate Sarah.
   b. I need to know for which girl x and for which boy y such that Mary ordered y to congratulate Sarah], x also ordered y to congratulate Sarah. [i.e., I need to know the girl-boy pairs such that both the girl and Mary ordered the boy to congratulate Sarah]

The first crucial comparison is (61a), glossed with its intended interpretation, (61b). Both (60a) and (61a) contain the same instance of ACD inside an in-situ *wh*-phrase in the middle DP position. In (60a) the *wh*-phrase that moved overtly came from a higher DP position. In (61a) the *wh*-phrase that moves overtly will come from the lower DP position. Thus, in (60a) ACD is not contained within an instance of *wh*-in-situ, but in (61a) it is. In my experience speakers uniformly find a sharp difference in the acceptability and interpretability of the two examples. Example (60a) is perhaps difficult to interpret, but (61a) is impossible.

Wh$_1$ in situ, ACD within wh$_1$
(61) a. *I need to know which girl Sue ordered [which boy that Mary (also) did Δ] to congratulate ____.
   b. I need to know for which girl *x* and [which boy *y* such that Mary ordered *y* to congratulate *x*], Sue also ordered *y* to congratulate *x*.   [i.e., I need to know the girl-boy pairs such that both Sue and Mary ordered the boy to congratulate the girl]

I conclude from the contrast between (60a) and (61a) that in apparent exceptions to the Superiority effect like (58b), *wh$_1$* does not undergo covert phrasal movement. Still, to assure ourselves that this explanation is both plausible and correct, we must construct other experiments that test other explanations of the contrast between (60a) and (61a). For example, one might ask whether the meaning of (61a) is in some way especially difficult to construct. This can be tested by examining constructions whose meaning is similar or identical to that of (61a), but whose syntax is different. Such experiments can be performed. Example (61a) involves a *wh*-phrase overtly moved from the third DP position. This *wh*-phrase binds an elided bound variable inside the second DP position. An equivalent interpretation can be obtained by switching the initial positions of the bound variable and the *wh*-phrase, and overtly moving *wh$_1$* (which now contains the second *wh*-phrase in situ). The relevant construction is (62), which expresses the meaning of (61a) but is quite acceptable. If there is any deviance to (62), it may be related to the failure of surface c-command between *which girl* and *her*, but the contrast with (61a) is sharp.

It's not the meaning of (61a) that renders it unacceptable ...
(62) ?[Which boy that Mary ordered to congratulate which girl] did Sue (also) order ____ to congratulate her?

As just noted, the interpretation of the elided VP in (61a) includes a variable bound by the overtly moved phrase *which girl*. This raises another possible account for the deviance of (61a). Might this variable within an elided VP obey the Complex NP Constraint, as a trace inside an overt VP would? That is, could the contrast between (60a) and (61a) stem from a violation of the Complex NP Constraint in (61a)? The answer seems to be no. Consider, for example, an instance of ACD that differs minimally from (61a) in that the position occupied by wh_1-in-situ in (61a) is occupied by a non-*wh*-phrase. An example is (63a), which replaces wh_1-in-situ with a quantified phrase headed by *every*. Since *every boy that Mary did* is not a *wh*-phrase, it does not compete with *which girl* for movement to C. Consequently, no special problem is expected with ACD—and none is found. Crucially, however, the ellipsis in (63a) contains a variable bound by *which girl* across a Complex NP Constraint boundary. Consequently, it is unlikely that this factor accounts for the unacceptability of (61a).

... nor is it the Complex NP Constraint violation within the ellipsis site ...

(63) a. I need to know which girl Sue ordered [every boy that Mary (also) did Δ] to congratulate ____.

   b. I need to know for which girl *x*, if Mary ordered a boy to congratulate *x*, then Sue also ordered that boy to congratulate *x*.

It is also worth verifying that if the *wh*-in-situ and the overtly moved *wh*-phrase are reversed (i.e., if the apparent Superiority violation is eliminated), ACD becomes acceptable. Though the example might (for some speakers) involve a Weak Crossover effect, the conclusion seems to be correct. Useful primes for (64a) are other sentences in which an in-situ *which*-phrase binds a variable to its left—for example, *Which man ordered a boy that liked her to congratulate which girl?*

... nor is it the apparent Superiority violation (wh_2 *in situ, ACD within overtly moved* wh_1*) ...*

(64) a. (?)I need to know [which boy that Mary (also) did Δ] Sue ordered ____ to congratulate which girl.

   b. I need to know for which girl *x* and [which boy *y* such that Mary ordered *y* to congratulate *x*], Sue also ordered *y* to congratulate *x*. [i.e., I need to know the girl-boy pairs such that both Sue and Mary ordered the boy to congratulate the girl]

Some other tests can be performed. For example, Hiroshi Aoyagi (personal communication) notes that it is important to make sure that the variable in wh_1 (inside the ellipsis site) in (61a) can in fact be bound by the overtly moved *wh*, as it needs to be. For example, one might ask whether wh_1 undergoes covert movement to a position *higher* than the overtly moved *wh*-phrase, making binding of a variable within wh_1 impossible for simple reasons of scope and c-command. Examples like (65), where the parasitic gap within the in-situ wh_1 is successfully bound by the moved *wh*-phrase, seem to suggest that this is not the case.

. . . nor is it binding into wh-*in-situ . . .*

(65) Which girl did you persuade [which friend of ____] to
    congratulate ____?

Another relevant example is due to James McCawley (personal communication). Example (66) is like (59), except that it has in common with (61a) a variable—here a pronoun—following wh_2-in-situ. Although McCawley actually judged the example deviant, I disagree.

. . . nor is it the variable bound by the moved wh *to the right of the* wh-*in-situ.*

(66) I need to know which girl ____ ordered [which boy that Bill (also)
    did Δ] to congratulate her.

In my view the tests performed here point to one clear conclusion. Whatever the syntactic fate of wh_1-in-situ in apparent Superiority violations like (58b), covert phrasal *wh*-movement is *not* one of the things that can happen to it. The next question, of course, is what *does* happen to wh_1-in-situ in such examples.

3.2   Covert Phrasal Movement and Case

Before turning to this question, however, I want to point out an interesting corollary result. The comparison between (60a) and (61a) has revealed a link between the availability of ACD inside a *wh*-phrase and the overall pattern of *wh*-movement: wh_1-in-situ in a multiple question does not undergo covert phrasal movement. Since it does not undergo covert phrasal movement, we can conclude a fortiori that it does not undergo covert phrasal *wh-movement*, which is our main concern here. But it is worth noting some implications of the stronger conclusion, because it bears directly on a current debate concerning the syntactic configurations that resolve ACD. If we consider the explanations for ACD resolution that have been offered in the literature and focus on those explanations that posit covert phrasal movement, we can distinguish two families of proposals.

One school of thought—represented, for example, by May (1985, 11–14)—argues that ACD resolution not only provides evidence of covert phrasal movement, but also reveals severe limitations on its distribution. We can call this school of thought the *limited movement* family of theories. In particular, May suggests that constraints on ACD show that covert phrasal movement is limited to special types of constituents—constituents whose special syntactic or interpretive needs motivate such movement. He takes the contrast between (67a) and (67b) to show that quantified expressions, but not DPs headed by proper names, undergo the covert phrasal movement that can resolve ACD.

Quantifiers versus proper names in ACD
(67) a. Dulles suspected [everyone who Angleton did Δ].
     b. *Dulles suspected [Philby, who Angleton did Δ].

May's explanation does not seem quite correct, however. The contrast between (67a) and (67b) does not seem to correlate directly with the quantificational nature of the relevant phrase, since focusing the VP inside the relative clause renders (67b) acceptable.

Focus eliminates the quantifier/proper name contrast
(68) a. Dulles suspected [Philby, who Angleton also did Δ].
     b. Dulles suspected [Philby, who Angleton did not Δ].
     c. Dulles did not suspect [Philby, who Angleton did Δ].

The contrast between (67b) and (68) is familiar from other cases of VP-ellipsis (or even simple VP-repetition, in some cases) and seems to be unrelated to ACD.[32]

Quantifier/proper name contrast not limited to ACD
(69) a. *Dulles suspected Philby. Angleton did Δ.
     b. Dulles suspected Philby. Angleton also did Δ.
     c. Dulles suspected Philby. Angleton did not Δ.
     d. Dulles did not suspect Philby. Angleton did Δ.

The real puzzle, then, is the absence of this focus requirement in restrictive relatives such as the one in (67a). I will not attempt to solve this puzzle here. In any case, Fiengo and May (1994, 242) note that a wide variety of NP types support ACD.

ACD with other NP types

(70) a. Dulles suspected some spy that Angleton did Δ.

    b. Dulles suspected the spy that Angleton did Δ.

    c. Dulles suspected many spies that Angleton did Δ.

These facts raise the question of whether, in Fiengo and May's words, "the construction can [still] be taken as a diagnostic for quantification." They suggest that it can. For example, they take (70b) to argue in favor of the Russellian analysis of definite descriptions as quantificational. And they note, with Diesing (1992) (though disagreeing over details), that the determiners in (70c) and similar examples receive a strong interpretation, which suggests some sort of QR-like operation on the object NP.

The other school of thought (which we can call the *Case movement* family of theories) rejects this conclusion. In particular, it abandons the view that the phrasal movement that resolves ACD in a direct object is limited to particular subtypes of DPs. According to this proposal, developed independently by Lasnik (1993) and Hornstein (1994, 1995), the covert phrasal movement that licenses ACD is not limited to "special DPs," but is actually a much more "garden-variety" type of movement— namely, movement for reasons of Case. Lasnik and Hornstein develop their proposals in the context of Chomsky's (1991, 1993) proposal that object Case is checked, not within VP, but in a VP-external projection (Agr$_O$P in Chomsky 1993; *v*P in Chomsky 1995) to which the object moves. They suggest that it is this kind of Case-driven movement, not QR or covert *wh*-movement, that resolves ACD in the standard cases.[33] (They develop this proposal as part of a broader proposal that QR does not exist, which I will not report here.)[34]

The central difference between the limited movement and the Case movement approaches lies in whether ACD resolution within direct objects is brought about by special processes that are limited to certain DP types (quantified phrases and *wh*-phrases), or whether ACD resolution is available to all direct object DPs that bear objective Case. Some of the arguments developed by Kennedy (1997) help answer this question, by arguing for the weak point that covert operations other than Case movement must at least be *allowed* to resolve ACD. As Kennedy notes, there are instances of ACD that require a type of movement that Case considerations do not motivate. For example, "NP-contained ACD" of the sort illustrated in (71) (Kennedy's (68)–(70)) has an interpretation entirely unexpected under theories in which ACD is resolved through Case movement.

NP-contained ACD
(71) a. Beck read [a report on [every suspect Kollberg did Δ]].
      b. Melander requested [copies of [most of the tapes Larsson did
         Δ]].
      c. Kollberg took [pictures of [the same people Beck did Δ]].

If any DP in (71) is assigned Case outside its VP, it is the external bracketed DP. However, the interpretation of ellipsis in these examples is
unexpected if ACD is resolved by Case movement. Instead, the interpretation is that derived if the *internal* bracketed DP undergoes covert
movement (e.g., QR) to a VP-external position.

LF representations for (71)
(72) a. [every suspect Kollberg read a report on]$_x$ Beck read a report
         on x
      b. [the tapes Larsson requested copies of]$_x$ Melander requested
         copies of most of x
      c. [Kollberg took pictures of the same people]$_x$ Beck took pictures
         of x

Thus, there must be some type of covert phrasal movement distinct from
Case movement that resolves ACD.[35]
   The contrast between (60a) and (61a) provides a good argument in
favor of an even stronger position. If objective Case really is checked
outside VP, through movement into Agr$_O$P or vP, this kind of movement cannot involve the entire object phrase, since it does not resolve
ACD. The point is straightforward. Examples (60a) and (61a), if I have
interpreted them correctly, display an interaction between *wh*-movement
and ACD resolution. More specifically, they show that when a lower
wh-phrase undergoes overt *wh*-movement past a higher direct object *wh*-
phrase, the higher phrase cannot contain an instance of ACD. If direct
object phrases uniformly undergo a type of movement for Case purposes
that is capable of resolving ACD, then the interaction with *wh*-movement
seen here could only entail (all things being equal) that movement of a
lower *wh*-phrase over a higher one prevents the higher *wh*-phrase from
undergoing movement for Case purposes. But this conclusion cannot be
correct. If objective Case cannot be checked on the higher *wh*-phrase, *wh*$_1$,
in these configurations, then—independent of ACD—such configurations
should have the status of Case Filter violations. But, of course, they do
not. Remove the ACD from (61a) and the structure, though complex,

does not violate the Case Filter, as (73) shows. Whatever might be wrong with (61a), Case is not the culprit.[36]

Wh₁-in-situ does not violate the Case Filter
(73) I need to know which girl Sue ordered which boy to
congratulate ____.

A limited movement hypothesis offers a more plausible perspective on the problem of (61a). Suppose only covert *phrasal wh*-movement can resolve ACD in a relative clause that modifies an in-situ interrogative *wh*-phrase. Though I have not yet explained why covert phrasal *wh*-movement is not available in these cases, the unavailability of such movement should not be surprising—even at this point in the story. After all, there *is* something special about wh_1-in-situ from the perspective of *wh*-movement. Furthermore, the hypothesis that wh_1-in-situ does not undergo covert phrasal *wh*-movement helps us understand the contrast between (61a) with ACD and (73) without ACD, since the presence of *phrasal* movement is crucial only to ACD.

Consequently, if Case on direct objects is checked external to VP,[37] the kind of direct object movement that accomplishes this task cannot be phrasal movement. Otherwise, whether or not wh_1-in-situ also undergoes phrasal *wh*-movement, Case movement alone would license ACD in examples like (61a). To put the matter differently: Hornstein (1994, 1995) and Lasnik (1993) were correct in noting that Case-driven phrasal movement to a VP-external position should license ACD, but they were wrong about the existence of this sort of phrasal movement.

Indeed, the conclusion that objective Case movement (if it exists) is not phrasal excludes not only proposals that posit that English direct objects undergo *covert* phrasal movement, but also proposals like Johnson's (1992) and Koizumi's (1995) that English direct objects undergo *overt* phrasal movement outside VP for Case reasons. The moment we posit *phrasal* object movement for Case reasons, we lose almost all hope of accounting for the ACD contrasts that concern us. Either there is no movement for Case purposes to a VP-external position, or there is only feature movement. The latter is, in fact, what Chomsky (1995) proposes.[38,39]

These conclusions from (60a) and (61a) fit quite nicely with arguments by Kennedy (1997) that also make the stronger case: not merely that operations like QR and covert *wh*-movement serve to resolve ACD, but also that covert objective Case movement does not. For example,

Kennedy notes (p. 675) that the *de dicto* reading normally available for the subject of an infinitive embedded under *want* disappears when that subject contains an elided VP whose antecedent is the VP headed by *want*. ((74a–b) are Kennedy's (50) and (48), respectively.)

De dicto *reading disappears*

(74) a. Kollberg [VP wants [everyone Beck wants to interrogate] to
         answer these questions].

    b. Kollberg [VP wants [everyone Beck does Δ] to answer these
         questions].

As Kennedy points out, (74a) "is ambiguous between a [*de re*] reading ... in which Kollberg's desire concerns particular individuals, and [a *de dicto*] one ... in which his desire concerns any individual who meets the requirements imposed by the restriction (that Beck wants to interrogate him)." By contrast, (74b) allows only the *de re*, "particular individual" reading. It cannot mean that Kollberg wants the set of people who answer the questions to coincide with the set of people who Beck wants to answer the questions, whoever that set may happen to consist of. In fact, as Danny Fox (personal communication) has pointed out, simpler examples can be constructed with bare DP objects.[40] These also display a *de re/de dicto* ambiguity eliminated by ACD.

De dicto *reading disappears*

(75) a. Kollberg [VP wanted [every book that Mary wrote]].

    b. Kollberg [VP wanted [every book Mary did Δ]].

In (75a) Kollberg might desire a particular set of books (without even knowing that they were written by the same person), or his desire may concern any book that Mary happens to have written. In (75b) Kollberg's desire must concern a particular set of books.

The data in (74)–(75) follow straightforwardly if ACD resolution requires covert phrasal movement of the bracketed phrase to a position that also happens to be outside the semantic scope of *want*. But this position cannot be the Case position for the bracketed DP; if it were, the *de dicto* reading would also be unavailable in (74a) and (75a), contrary to fact. Therefore, the Case position for the embedded subject, wherever it is, must have two properties: (1) it lies within the scope of *want*, and (2) movement to it does not license ACD resolution.[41]

Chapter 4

What Does Happen to Wh_1-in-Situ?

4.1 Does Wh_1-in-Situ Undergo Feature Movement?

In previous chapters, I have argued that in D-linked exceptions to the Superiority effect, wh_1-in-situ does not undergo covert phrasal movement. This argument is possible only because the ACD behavior of wh_1-in-situ can be contrasted with the behavior of wh-in-situ that do undergo covert phrasal movement. So far this conclusion accords with the argument in Pesetsky 1987 that wh_1-in-situ fails to undergo covert phrasal movement.[42] At this point, however, the work of the last few years raises new questions. In Pesetsky 1987, I assumed that if an in-situ wh-phrase fails to undergo covert phrasal movement, it undergoes no movement at all. For that reason I suggested that a special mechanism (unselective binding) assigns such wh-in-situ their scope, but that no instance of wh-movement applies to them. Now, however, a less ad hoc proposal is possible. In particular, we can ask whether a wh-in-situ that fails to undergo wh-phrase movement might nonetheless undergo wh-feature movement. In (58b), for example (*Which book did which person buy ____?*), even though wh_1, *which person*, fails to undergo covert phrasal wh-movement, could it be that its wh-feature has moved on its own to the interrogative $C_{\text{m-spec}}$, leaving the rest of the phrase behind?

This possibility suggests a new perspective on apparent exceptions to the Superiority effect. (I call them "apparent exceptions" from this point on.) Perhaps wh_1-in-situ in these examples actually undergoes wh-feature movement. If so, we might entertain the possibility that this instance of feature movement is actually the *first* instance of wh-movement in its clause—the first instance of overt phrasal movement actually constituting the *second* instance of wh-movement overall. On this view the pronunciation principle for English wh-movement remains accurate in exactly the form given earlier. The first instance of *phrasal* movement is overt, even if the first instance of phrasal *wh*-movement is not the first instance of *wh*-movement.

Feature movement analysis of apparent exceptions to the Superiority effect
(76) a. *Structure before movement*
       $C_{\text{m-spec}}$ [which person bought which book]
    b. *Step 1*
       $C_{\text{m-spec}}$ attracts the *wh*-feature of *which person*
       F_i-C [F_i-which person bought which book]
    c. *Step 2*
       $C_{\text{m-spec}}$ attracts the *wh*-phrase *which book*
       which book F_i-C [F_i-which person bought ____]
    d. *Pronounced result*
       Which book did which person buy?

If this hypothesis is correct, then—although such examples sound as if they violate Attract Closest (AC)—in reality AC is not violated at all. The first *wh*-feature attracted by $C_{\text{m-spec}}$ in the course of the derivation is the closest instance of this feature. The only relevant difference between *Which book did which person buy* ____? and *Which person* ____ *bought which book?* lies in whether the first instance of *wh*-movement is feature movement or phrasal movement.

This hypothesis, in turn, raises the possibility that AC for the *wh*-feature is inviolable, just as Chomsky (1995) suggests.[43] The appearance of counterexamples arises simply from the failure to consider the possibility that the first instance of overt movement to $C_{\text{m-spec}}$ might not be the first instance of movement to $C_{\text{m-spec}}$. On this hypothesis the failure of ACD in a relative clause attached to wh_1-in-situ[44] (as seen in (61a)) stems from the same cause as the failure of ACD in relative clauses attached to the associate of *there*, studied earlier in connection with (25). In each case movement takes place from the constituent that contains ACD, but because the movement is not phrasal, ACD is not resolved.

4.2   What Is Special about Questions with D-Linking?

This proposal comes no closer than previous efforts to explaining why the semantic property of D-linking yields an exception to the Superiority effect in (76), but it suggests a new way of looking at the syntactic side of the problem. Nothing so far has excluded the possibility of a derivation like (76) for English examples without D-linking—yet these do show a Superiority effect. We need to know what is wrong with a derivation like (77).

Spurious derivation of an apparent exception to Superiority

(77) a. *Structure before movement*
   $C_{m\text{-spec}}$ [who bought what]
   b. *Step 1*
   $C_{m\text{-spec}}$ attracts the *wh*-feature of *who*
   F_i-C [F_i-who bought what]
   c. *Step 2*
   $C_{m\text{-spec}}$ attracts the *wh*-phrase *what*
   what F_i-C [F_i-who bought ____]
   d. *Pronounced result*
   *What did who buy?

I want to suggest that what is wrong with (77) is that it violates a constraint we have already seen in a different form in Bulgarian: the multiple-specifier requirement of $C_{m\text{-spec}}$ presented in (36), repeated here.

Multiple-specifier requirement of $C_{m\text{-spec}}$

(78) $C_{m\text{-spec}}$ requires more than one *wh*-specifier.

Recall that this requirement displays itself in Bulgarian as the strong requirement that at least two *wh*-phrases undergo overt phrasal movement in a multiple question. If a multiple question involves only two *wh*-phrases, and one of them undergoes feature movement to C, the multiple-specifier requirement cannot be satisfied. This, I suggest, is what goes wrong with the derivation sketched in (77). Feature movement involves communication between the *wh*-feature of *who* and a corresponding feature of $C_{m\text{-spec}}$, but it does not involve copying a phrase into a specifier position, which could help satisfy the multiple-specifier requirement.[45]

If this idea is correct, then the multiple-specifier requirement must somehow be suspended in questions that involve D-linking; if it is not, the derivation in (76) will also lead to deviance. Let us suppose that this is the case.

Multiple-specifier requirement of $C_{m\text{-spec}}$ (revised)

(79) Except in questions where a *wh*-phrase is D-linked, $C_{m\text{-spec}}$ requires more than one *wh*-specifier.

Alternatively, D-linked multiple questions might be formed (and receive normal "pair-list" readings) with the complementizer otherwise reserved for nonmultiple questions: the interrogative complementizer $C_{1\text{-spec}}$ that takes only one *wh*-phrase as specifier. On this view we would not need the exception clause built into (79), but we would need to understand why the semantics of D-linked multiple questions allows a complementizer that is otherwise not found in such questions. I do not know at present how to decide between the two hypotheses.[46]

More generally, it remains unclear why D-linked phrases should constitute an exception to the multiple-specifier requirement. In this domain my proposal leaves an important question unanswered. This is not grounds for giving up on the proposal, however. Even when one is forced to leave some aspect of a phenomenon unexplained, one can often tell whether the discussion is on the right track by examining whether the unexplained portion of the phenomenon has internal coherence. If so, there are grounds for optimism about the overall approach—grounds for suspecting that the unanswered question is a real question about the true theory and not merely an artifact of missteps and false notions. In the present case, if the absence of Superiority effects with D-linked *wh* in English is due to an exception to the multiple-specifier requirement, we immediately expect this exception to show up in a slightly different way in Bulgarian. In English the multiple-specifier requirement, combined with the pronunciation principles stated earlier, produces one overt occurrence of *wh*-phrase movement and one covert occurrence. In Bulgarian the multiple-specifier requirement, combined with the pronunciation principles for that language, forces the *overt* fronting of at least two *wh*-phrases. Consequently, if the D-linking exception to English Superiority effects arises from an exception to the multiple-specifier requirement, we expect D-linking to improve Bulgarian multiple questions in which just one *wh*-phrase has fronted. As mentioned in note 24, this is the case. Examples like the double-asterisked (35d), (40d), and (41d), in which only one out of three or four *wh*-phrases has fronted, are significantly improved when one or the other *wh*-phrase is understood as D-linked (i.e., as demanding answers drawn from a set that counts as old information for speaker and hearer). The same is true of questions with only two *wh*-phrases ("binary questions"). ((80) is from Roumyana Izvorski (personal communication).)

D-linked wh-*in-situ (Bulgarian)*

(80) a. Koj dade kakvo na Stefan?   [* if non-D-linked; better if D-linked]
      who gave what to Stefan
   b. Koj kakvo dade na Stefan?   [no D-linking preference]

Furthermore, as mentioned in note 19, a binary question may constitute an exception to Superiority, so long as the question involves D-linking—just as in English.

D-linking exception to Superiority in questions with overt movement (Bulgarian)
(81) Kakvo koj dade na Stefan?   [* if non-D-linked; better if D-linked]

If I am correct in my suppositions about *wh*-feature movement, (81) receives an analysis akin to (76), the multiple-specifier requirement becoming irrelevant because of the D-linking exception.[47]

4.3 Nonbinary Multiple Questions

As it happens, in Pesetsky 1987 (citing Wachowicz 1974 and Jae-Woong Choe, personal communication) the Polish counterpart of the just-cited Bulgarian facts was used as an argument for the hypothesis that D-linked *wh*-in-situ may fail to undergo covert phrasal *wh*-movement. In the context of that work, questions with D-linking were not an exception to a multiple-specifier requirement, but an exception to a proposed requirement that each *wh*-phrase undergo some form of phrasal *wh*-movement by LF. I viewed Polish as a language that "wears its LF on its sleeve," thanks to the phenomenon of multiple overt *wh*-phrase movement. The discussion had certain marked deficiencies, however. For its conclusions to have force, it was necessary to assume that Polish *wh*-movement is always overt (an assumption I did not make explicit). Furthermore (needless to say) the possibility of feature movement was not considered at all. In this context it was reasonable to assume that D-linking is an exception to a movement requirement for *wh*-phrases, rather than an exception to a requirement on the specifiers of $C_{m\text{-spec}}$.

In fact, however, evidence now available favors the latter view over the former. Recall that the multiple-specifier requirement is satisfied once two *wh*-phrases have moved to [Spec, $C_{m\text{-spec}}$]. Superiority effects arise in binary questions without D-linking because such questions contain only two *wh*-phrases in the first place. Consequently, a derivation in which one of the two *wh*-phrases undergoes feature movement inevitably violates the multiple-specifier requirement. The situation should be different, however, in a multiple question that contains *more than two wh*-phrases. In such a question, nothing said so far should block a derivation in which one or more of the *wh*-phrases undergoes *wh*-feature movement, so long as at least two *wh*-phrases undergo the phrasal version of *wh*-movement. In particular, in a question with three or more *wh*-phrases, wh_1 (the highest *wh*-phrase) should be able to undergo *wh*-feature movement as the first instance of *wh*-movement (satisfying AC), with two of the lower *wh*-phrases undergoing phrasal movement. Of these instances of phrasal movement, the first will be overt in English, and the rest will be covert. In other words, independent of D-linking, questions with three or more *wh*-phrases should show no Superiority effect. In fact, this is the case, as I pointed out when presenting example (33), repeated here.

Superiority effect disappears with more than two wh-*phrases*
(82) a. *What did who give ____ to Mary?   [detectable Superiority effect]
     b. What did who give ____ to whom?   [no detectable Superiority effect]

Example (82a) contains only two *wh*-phrases. Consequently, both must undergo phrasal *wh*-movement, in order to satisfy the multiple-specifier requirement of $C_{m\text{-spec}}$. Since AC is inviolable, *who* must move first, and *what* second. By the pronunciation principles, movement of *who* should be the overt instance of movement. Since this not the case in (82a), the sentence is deviant. Example (82b), on the other hand, contains three *wh*-phrases. The highest *wh*-phrase, *who*, is thus free to undergo *wh*-feature movement, as the first instance of *wh*-movement to the complementizer of the question. *What* and *whom* then undergo phrasal *wh*-movement, satisfying the multiple-specifier requirement. The first instance of *wh*-movement is overt, and the result is (82b).

The disappearance of Superiority effects with nonbinary multiple questions makes it clear that the grammar of multiple questions contains a multiple-specifier requirement, and not a requirement that all *wh*-phrases undergo phrasal *wh*-movement. This, in turn, tells us exactly which property of grammar D-linked questions are exceptions to. Despite our ignorance concerning the semantic source of this D-linking exception, the strong hidden parallels between Bulgarian and English revealed by this approach suggest that we are on the right track. The failure of D-linked questions to display the Superiority effect in English groups with the fact that D-linking in Bulgarian obviates the requirement that two *wh*-phrases move overtly. The fact that English questions with more than two *wh*-phrases also fail to show the Superiority effect groups with the fact that Bulgarian multiple questions with two overtly moved *wh*-phrases are significantly better than multiple questions with only one overtly moved *wh*-phrase.

An additional observation may support this perspective. From time to time I have encountered speakers of English who report a residual Superiority effect in those cases where other speakers report its disappearance. For these speakers the Superiority contrast weakens in questions with D-linking and in nonbinary multiple questions, but it remains detectable. It is not implausible that this "lesser" Superiority contrast reflects the effect in English of Bulgarian's "general preference" reported in (37) for multiple questions in which all *wh*-phrases are attracted to $C_{m\text{-spec}}$. If my proposals are correct, apparent Superiority violations always involve at least one *wh*-phrase (wh_1) undergoing feature movement, rather than phrasal movement, to $C_{m\text{-spec}}$.[48]

The same considerations may help us understand comparable cases in Bulgarian. The Superiority effect in Bulgarian shows up as the observation that where wh_1 has clearly undergone overt *wh*-movement, it is leftmost among the *wh*-phrases that have fronted. We have already seen this effect in binary questions in (43)–(44). The same effect can be observed in ternary questions. Where it is clear that wh_1 has undergone overt *wh*-phrase movement, it must be leftmost among the various *wh*-phrases. Examples (83a–b) must be parsed either with *koj* 'who' in situ, violating the multiple-specifier requirement, or with *koj* having undergone overt *wh*-phrase movement later than a lower *wh*-phrase, violating AC. That is why these examples are completely unacceptable.

Violation of multiple-specifier requirement or violation of AC
(83) a. **Na kogo   koj   dade kakvo?
              to   whom who gave what
       b. **Kakvo koj dade na kogo?

Such examples contrast detectably with minimally different (though still unacceptable) examples in which *koj* is arguably completely in situ. Although one may remain skeptical of arguments based on a contrast between strong and weaker unacceptability ("**" vs. "*"), the contrast here is apparently quite clear.[49]

Multiple-specifier requirement satisfied/AC satisfied
(84) *Na kogo   kakvo dade koj?
           to   whom what gave who

If my hypothesis is correct, the first instance of *wh*-movement to $C_{m\text{-spec}}$ in (84) is *wh*-feature movement from *koj*. The second instance of *wh*-

movement involves the *wh*-phrase that ends up leftmost, and the third instance of *wh*-movement involves the second overtly fronted *wh*-phrase. The contrast between (83) and (84) follows as the Bulgarian counterpart to the English difference between binary and nonbinary multiple questions that appear to violate Superiority. Of course, (84) is not fully acceptable, as the asterisk indicates. This fact may reflect the preference for multiple questions in which all *wh*-phrases undergo *wh*-phrase movement (especially if this preference is stronger for Bulgarian speakers, who can hear the difference, than it is for English speakers).[50]

One final empirical point must be investigated. The proposal in this section has presupposed that wh_1-in-situ in non-D-linked ternary questions has essentially the same syntax as its counterpart in D-linked binary questions. That is, it fails to undergo phrasal *wh*-movement—but it does undergo *wh*-feature movement, if my hypothesis is correct. ACD evidence bearing on this point is hard to come by. In order to construct a fair test, we need to avoid D-linking, and we need at least four argument places to work with (in order to vary the status of the *wh*-phrase with ACD from wh_1-in-situ to wh_2-in-situ while holding other conditions constant). To the extent that such examples can be constructed, and to the extent that they do not pose insuperable burdens on linguistic memory, the facts appear to be as expected. It is exceedingly difficult to parse (85a–b), but insofar as one can judge the examples at all, they seem to contrast as indicated. Example (85b) suffers from the repetition of *who*, but its instance of ACD seems to be interpretable, unlike ACD in (85a). The problem with the judgment is the excessive concentration required to deliver it.

ACD in wh_1 *within three-wh questions*
(85) a. *What did Sue order [who that Mary (also) did Δ] to give ____ to whom?
     b. What did who order [who that Mary (also) did Δ] to give ____ to whom?[51]

4.4 Wh-Feature Movement versus No Wh-Movement at All

The discussion in sections 4.1–4.3 has provided only one real argument that directly bears on the existence of *wh*-feature movement. This was the observation that if *wh*-feature movement can be the first instance of *wh*-movement, examples that look like violations of AC really do not violate it at all. If we accept the evidence from the *there* construction in favor of the existence of nonphrasal feature movement, this consideration is significant, since it explains the existence of apparent Superiority violations as a consequence of independently detected properties of grammar. In this sense it is superior to certain potential alternatives.

For example, one might suppose that the *wh*-phrases that undergo *wh*-feature movement (according to my hypotheses) are actually "invisible" to *wh*-attraction by $C_{m\text{-spec}}$ and undergo no *wh*-movement whatsoever. On this view, so long as the multiple-specifier requirement is satisfied in the end, an invisible wh_1 would be free to remain overlooked by *wh*-attraction. The multiple-specifier requirement would filter out non-D-linked binary questions in which one of the two *wh*-phrases had been marked invisible.[52] The cost of this proposal, however, would be the postulation of a construction-specific "invisibility" motivated only by apparent Superiority violations. The feature movement proposal may be the less complex of the two—but more evidence bearing on the issue would still be welcome.

It is clear what we want to find out. We know from ACD that in apparent Superiority violations, wh_1 undergoes neither overt nor covert phrasal *wh*-movement. Can we tell whether it undergoes any sort of *wh*-movement—in particular, feature movement? More specifically, do we have a tool for detecting whether wh_1-in-situ undergoes feature movement before the first instance of overt phrasal *wh*-movement?

Surprisingly, we do have such a tool. One might think it impossible to distinguish between phonologically vacuous feature movement and the absence of movement, but we can actually do so by looking at the impact that feature movement should have on other, later operations that do have phonological consequences. Richards's (1997) Principle of Minimal Compliance (PMC), discussed in section 2.2, provides just the tool we need to detect this impact.[53]

Recall how I introduced this principle. Following Richards (who in turn used evidence from Bošković 1995, 1999), I noted that the first instance of *wh*-movement in a Bulgarian multiple question has a notable effect on subsequent instances of *wh*-movement within that multiple question. In particular, once overt *wh*-phrase movement has taken place in accordance with AC, subsequent instances of *wh*-phrase movement do not need to satisfy AC.[54] As I discussed, and as illustrated in derivation (49), repeated here as (87), it is as if satisfying AC with the initial instance of movement to $C_{m\text{-spec}}$ pays an "AC tax" that provides immunity to AC for other instances of *wh*-movement to that $C_{m\text{-spec}}$. As a consequence, orders like wh_1 wh_2 wh_3 and wh_1 wh_3 wh_2 are nearly equal in acceptability, as (46), repeated as (86), shows.

Wh$_1$ wh$_2$ wh$_3$ *and* wh$_1$ wh$_3$ wh$_2$ *both acceptable (Bulgarian)*
(86) a. Koj na kogo   kakvo dade?
          who to whom what   gave
          'Who gave what to whom?'
    b. ?Koj kakvo na kogo dade?

Demonstration of "AC tax"
(87) a. *Before* wh-*movement*
          C$_{\text{m-spec}}$ [koj dade na kogo kakvo]
    b. *Step 1*
          C$_{\text{m-spec}}$ attracts the *wh*-feature of *koj* (wh_1), pays "AC tax."
          koj C [_____ dade na kogo kakvo]
    c. *Step 2*
          C$_{\text{m-spec}}$ attracts either of the remaining *wh*-phrases, since "AC tax" has been paid. *Wh*-phrase tucks in under *koj*.
          koj kakvo C [_____ dade na kogo _____]
    d. *Step 3*
          C$_{\text{m-spec}}$ attracts the other *wh*-phrase, which tucks in under *kakvo*.
          koj kakvo na kogo C [_____ dade _____ _____]

This effect, if I have understood it correctly, provides a way of telling whether an instance of overt *wh*-movement in an English multiple question is the first or the second instance in its clause. If overt *wh*-movement in English has been preceded by another type of *wh*-movement, it should show no effects of AC, since the earlier instance of *wh*-movement has already paid an "AC tax." On the other hand, if the overt *wh*-movement in a particular multiple question is the first instance of *wh*-movement, it should show the effects of AC.

Consider in particular a question with three *wh*-phrases: wh_1, wh_2, and wh_3. By the multiple-specifier requirement, we know that at least two of them must undergo phrasal movement. As a factual matter, we know that questions with three *wh*-phrases may appear to violate Superiority. Consider such a case. By hypothesis, wh_1 does not undergo phrasal movement at all, but wh_2 and wh_3 do. The question is, which one undergoes phrasal movement first?

If we suppose that apparent Superiority violations are allowed because wh_1 can be marked as "invisible" to movement, then what we hear as overt *wh*-movement is the first instance of *wh*-movement in its clause. This instance of movement would have to involve wh_2, because wh_2 is the closest *attractable wh*-phrase. (If wh_2 were marked as "invisible," the first instance of *wh*-movement would involve wh_3, but the structure would be filtered out by the multiple-specifier requirement.) Consequently, apparent Superiority violations in questions with three *wh*-phrases would need to show wh_2 overtly moved and wh_3 remaining in situ. On the other hand, if apparent Superiority violations arise simply because wh_1 may undergo *wh*-feature movement, then this instance of feature movement is expected to pay the "AC tax" for its multiple question. The next instance of *wh*-movement must be phrasal, or else the multiple-specifier requirement would not be satisfied in the end. This instance of *wh*-movement will also be overt. But because the "AC tax" has already been paid, we expect both wh_2 and wh_3 to be possible candidates for the overt instance of *wh*-movement.

The facts support the feature movement proposal. In ternary questions with wh_1-in-situ, either wh_2 or wh_3 may undergo overt *wh*-movement. The only interfering factor is a slight dispreference for sequences of identical *wh*-phrases in these structures. This factor degrades sequences like *who did who* ... As the pair of paradigms (88)–(89) show, this dispreference crosscuts the effect under investigation. In (88) it favors overt movement of wh_2, but in (89) it favors overt movement of wh_3.[55]

Wh_1 wh_2 wh_3 *and* wh_1 wh_3 wh_2 *both acceptable (English)*

(88) a.   Who ____ gave what to whom?   [wh_1 moves overtly]

   b.   What did who give ____ to whom?   [wh_2 moves overtly]

   c.   ?Who did who give what to ____?   [wh_3 moves overtly]

(89) a.   Who ____ persuaded whom to buy what?   [wh_1 moves overtly]

   b.   ?Who did who persuade ____ to buy what?   [wh_2 moves overtly]

   c.   What did who persuade whom to buy ____?   [wh_3 moves overtly]

The derivation of (89c) proceeds as follows:

Derivation of (89c)

(90) a. *Before* wh-*movement*

   $C_{m\text{-}spec}$ [who persuaded whom to buy what]

b. *Step 1*
   C attracts the *wh*-feature of *who* (wh_1), pays "AC tax" (PMC).
   F_i-C [F_i-who persuaded whom to buy what]

c. *Step 2*
   C attracts either of the remaining *wh*-phrases, since the PMC no
   longer requires obedience to AC.
   what F_i-C [F_i-who persuaded whom to buy ____]

d. *Step 3*
   C attracts the other *wh*-phrase.
   what whom F_i-C [F_i-who persuaded ____ to buy ____]

e. *Pronounced result*
   What did who persuade whom to buy?

The free choice of which *wh*-phrase moves overtly in ternary questions
with wh_1-in-situ is thus essentially the same fact as the free choice of
which *wh*-phrase moves *second* in Bulgarian overt phrasal movement. (In
addition, (84) has already displayed an example in Bulgarian of the derivation now being considered in English—an example in which the first
instance of *wh*-movement is feature movement in a Bulgarian multiple
question.) We thus have support for the hypothesis that in apparent
Superiority violations in English, the first instance of *wh*-movement is
actually feature movement—specifically, feature movement that satisfies
AC.[56] Thus, apparent exceptions to the Superiority effect, when examined
more closely, are really not exceptions at all.

This evidence also bears on an issue I have not discussed so far. I posed
the problem of explaining apparent violations of AC. My proposal has
the interesting consequence that these violations are merely apparent. AC
is being satisfied by an instance of *wh*-movement that had not previously
been postulated. (The alternative involving "invisibility" also had this
property.) I might have chosen to consider another possibility: that
apparent violations of AC really do violate this constraint. One approach
of this kind might use the logic of Optimality Theory (OT; Prince and
Smolensky 1993), in which certain constraints on linguistic form can be
violated when this is the only way to satisfy other, more highly valued
(highly ranked) constraints. If the apparent Superiority violations discussed here were actual AC violations, one would not expect to discover
the evidence I have presented that these violations are merely apparent.[57]
In particular, one would be surprised to see AC violated in ternary questions, with no apparent pressure on output forms to minimize this viola-

tion by preferring overt movement of the second closest *wh*-phrase in cases where the first closest cannot (for some reason) move. Consequently, this set of apparent violations does not provide support for the view that constraints on movement are ranked and violable in an OT fashion.

This observation is of interest, since proposals that tend in the opposite direction (for different sets of data) have been advanced in a number of studies, including Grimshaw 1997 and many papers in Barbosa et al. 1998. In Pesetsky 1997, 1998, I suggested that those OT interactions that are visible in syntactic phenomena actually reflect the way in which phonology interprets syntax (e.g., via the pronunciation principles discussed earlier), and I speculated that principles governing movement might not be ranked and violable in an OT fashion. My current proposal about apparent Superiority violations removes a case that might have seemed to support the opposing view.[58] As far as I can tell, except for the effects of the PMC, AC is inviolable. In addition, I can draw a methodological moral: exceptions and violations are not necessarily what they appear to be. More takes place in syntax than meets the ear.[59]

4.5 Interim Summary

The central argument for my proposal concerning feature movement comes from the fact that the peculiarities of English multiple questions turn out to faithfully reproduce the peculiarities of Bulgarian multiple questions if the feature movement proposal is assumed. The only difference we must posit between Bulgarian and English multiple questions concerns the pronunciation of *wh*-phrase movement structures (i.e., how many instances of *wh*-phrase movement to a given $C_{m\text{-spec}}$ are overt; see (56)–(57)). Otherwise, the syntax of multiple questions is identical in the two languages. I am now in a position to summarize this result. (Relevant example numbers are given after each comment.)

The multiple-specifier requirement of $C_{m\text{-spec}}$
In a non-D-linked question, at least two *wh*-phrases must be attracted by $C_{m\text{-spec}}$.
Bulgarian: In a non-D-linked binary question, at least two *wh*-phrases move overtly. This is clear from the distribution of overt *wh*-fronting. (35), (40), (41)
English: In a non-D-linked binary question, *wh*-feature movement is not an option for either *wh*-phrase. This cannot be viewed directly (though

ACD shows that the in-situ *wh may* undergo covert *wh*-phrase movement), but it is crucial to the distribution of Superiority effects, as indicated in what follows.

The Superiority effect
In a non-D-linked binary question, where the multiple-specifier requirement forces both *wh*-phrases to undergo *wh*-phrase movement, wh_1 moves first.
Bulgarian: In a non-D-linked binary question, both *wh*-phrases are overtly fronted and wh_1 is leftmost (given the "tucking in" property enforced by Shortest Move). (43)–(44), (83)
English: In a non-D-linked binary question, one *wh*-phrase is overtly fronted; the other is covertly fronted. Wh_1 is the overtly fronted *wh*. (26)–(27)

The D-linked exception to the multiple-specifier requirement
In a D-linked question, there is no requirement that at least two *wh*-phrases must be attracted by $C_{m\text{-spec}}$. This means that wh_1 might undergo feature movement.
Bulgarian: In a D-linked question, it is not necessary that at least two *wh*-phrases move overtly. (80)
English: In a D-linked binary question, *wh*-feature movement is an option for either *wh*-phrase. (76)

The absence of Superiority effects in questions with D-linking
Bulgarian: In a D-linked question, wh_1 may remain in situ. (81)
English: In a D-linked binary question, wh_1 may remain in situ. (31)–(32)   [ACD shows that it does not undergo covert phrasal movement. (60)–(61)]

The absence of Superiority effects with nonbinary questions
When a multiple question contains more than two *wh*-phrases, wh_1 may undergo *wh*-feature movement, so long as at least two *wh*-phrases undergo *wh*-phrase movement.
Bulgarian: In a ternary question, wh_1 may be pronounced in situ. (83)–(84)
English: In a ternary question, wh_1 may be pronounced in situ. (33)/(82)

The PMC and AC
Once a first instance of *wh*-movement to a given C has obeyed AC, subsequent instances need not obey AC.

Bulgarian: In a ternary question, in which wh_1 has moved overtly and is the leftmost moved *wh*-phrase, the order of subsequent *wh*-phrases is free. (46)–(48) [Also: when wh_1 undergoes feature movement and is pronounced in situ, the choice of leftmost overtly moved *wh* is free. (84)] *English:* When wh_1 undergoes feature movement and is pronounced in situ, the choice of overtly moved *wh* is free. (88)–(89)

The next two sections take up (inconclusively) some loose ends. In particular, I want to examine a few possible competitors to the "feature movement" hypothesis, in part to note their advantages and disadvantages, but most important, to show that my overall account is compatible with a variety of hypotheses concerning the true nature of what I have been calling "feature movement." I then move on to a deeper discussion of the specifier potential of interrogative complementizers.

4.6   Is "Feature Movement" Really *Feature* Movement?

One possible competitor to the "feature movement" hypothesis is relevant to an issue left open in the discussion so far: the choice between phrasal and feature movement in a derivation. Consider what happens when $C_{m\text{-spec}}$ has been introduced into a structure and proceeds to attract instances of the *wh*-feature to it. I have suggested that this attraction may proceed in either of two ways: either the feature itself is attracted from an expression that bears it, or the largest phrase that bears the feature is copied as a specifier of $C_{m\text{-spec}}$. I have also noted that certain properties of the attractor—properties *external* to the laws of movement—dictate which type of attraction occurs in a particular case. External properties include the fact that $C_{m\text{-spec}}$ requires two specifiers and the fact that $C_{1\text{-spec}}$ requires one, facts I will explore in greater detail in the next chapter.

Are there other, more general preferences for one type of movement over the other, rooted in the laws of movement, in addition to "external" filters that may require phrasal movement in certain circumstances? As noted earlier, Chomsky (1995) answers this question in the affirmative. He suggests that attraction of the *smallest* possible unit—the feature itself—is a more economical operation than attraction of any larger unit. The basis for Chomsky's particular claim is the idea that feature movement is the proper reanalysis of covert phrasal movement—coupled with the claim (inherited from earlier work) that covert movement is the default. I have argued throughout this book against the first of these claims. As noted earlier, it is not clear whether there is any particular reason to hold to the second claim, though it can certainly be modified to be consistent with the present discussion.

Still, it is worth mentioning variant proposals that might be equally appealing in other ways. For example, consider the observation that words and phrases bear grammatical features by virtue of their introduction as a subconstituent of these words and phrases. In the case of English *wh*-words, it is not implausible to imagine that the *wh*-feature is introduced by means of the *wh*-morpheme /h^w/ with which these words begin. (The fact that two English "*wh*-words" actually begin with pronounced /h/ is plausibly a reflex of the phonological processes mentioned below.) In several cases the morpheme that follows /h^w/ also appears in a demonstrative whose initial morpheme is /ð/.[60]

The English wh-*morpheme*

(91) h^wʌt 'what'   (many speakers lose aspiration)   cf. *that*
      h^wen 'when'   "   cf. *then*
      h^weyr 'where'   "   cf. *there*
      h^way 'why'   "
      h^wɪč 'which'   "
      h^waw 'how'   (with dissimilative loss of rounding;
                           cf. the absence of /k^waw . . ./)[61]
      h^w 'who'   (with the rounding feature appearing
                           on epenthetic vowel)

The morpheme /h^w/ is cognate with /k/ in Bulgarian and other Slavic languages. Slavic *wh*-morpheme /k/ alternates rather regularly with demonstrative /s/, much as English /h^w/ alternates with demonstrative /ð/. Other, unrelated languages—for example, Japanese—show similar patterns.

The Japanese wh-*morpheme*

(92) dore 'which one'   cf. kore 'this one'   sore   are 'that one'[62]
      dono 'which'   cf. kono 'this'   sono   ano 'that'
      dotira 'whither'   cf. kotira 'this direction' sotira atira 'that direction'
      doo 'how'   cf. koo 'this manner'   soo   — 'that manner'
      dare 'who'   cf. kare 'he'   —   —

If the "*wh*"-morpheme in languages like English, Bulgarian, and Japanese has no grammatical properties besides its role as the bearer of the *wh*-feature, *wh*-feature movement might simply be the attraction of this morpheme from inside the word that contains it (see Watanabe's (1992) and Tsai's (1994) proposals along similar lines). One might ask whether other instances of "feature movement" might be better viewed as "morpheme movement"—though obvious questions arise where a phonologically distinct morpheme cannot be identified (e.g., nominative Case in English). If this proposal is correct, then feature movement is simply the copying of a morphosyntactic constituent, just like more familiar examples of movement.[63] When *wh*-feature movement takes place from a phrase like *which book* or *who*, it is the *wh*-morpheme that is being copied to C (perhaps adjoining to it). The movement is *covert* in that the morpheme remains pronounced in its original position. This may simply reflect its status as a bound morpheme. If this view is correct, then "feature movement" is movement of the *smallest* unit that bears the feature in question.[64]

AC raises some obvious questions if "feature movement" is morpheme movement. The *wh*-feature present in *wh*-words is also present in larger "*wh*-phrases" that contain these words, at least insofar as attraction of *wh* may attract a phrase containing the morpheme—the "phrasal movement" I have discussed throughout.[65] Crucially, it is the distance from $C_{m\text{-spec}}$ to the maximal *wh*-phrase—not the distance from $C_{m\text{-spec}}$ to the *wh*-morpheme—that counts for the calculation of "closeness" relevant to AC, even when the maximal phrase, rather than the minimal unit, is copied.

Closeness

(93) A feature β is *closer* to K than α iff K c-commands an occurrence of β, and β asymmetrically c-commands an occurrence of α.

Phrasal movement can now be seen as copying the closest bearer of the relevant feature. Feature movement, by contrast, can now be seen as copying the smallest bearer of a feature. As suggested by Norvin Richards in work in progress, and as mentioned earlier in this book, both conditions—closeness and smallness—fit the spirit of "economy." Either is a plausible candidate for a genuine principle of grammar. Quite possibly, movement is possible if it meets either one.[66] Putting the matter in procedural terms, the target scans down the tree for the closest occurrence of the feature it attracts. When it finds an occurrence on a constituent, it has a choice: it either copies that constituent or copies the smallest subconstituent that contains the feature. Excluded is copying of an intermediate constituent that bears the relevant feature, since it is neither the closest nor the smallest expression of the relevant feature.

It is entirely possible, of course, that other considerations will come to light that restrict the choice between feature (morpheme) movement and phrasal movement. For example, feature movement for Case purposes may be intrinsically preferred over phrasal movement. I was able to demonstrate the properties of feature movement successfully with the *there* construction in part because (evidently) covert phrasal movement to T is impossible in this construction. In discussing ACD in multiple questions, I showed that covert phrasal movement to a VP-external objective Case position is impossible. (Overt phrasal movement to subject position is the consequence of other considerations, often grouped under the rubric "Extended Projection Principle.") Conceivably, these two observations reveal that preferences for feature movement over phrasal movement exist. The question would be whether this preference is limited to movement for Case purposes, or whether the preference is more general, in the spirit of Chomsky's (1995) proposals. For now I take these to be open questions.

4.7 Is "Feature Movement" Really Feature *Movement*?

Another open question concerns island effects. When I first introduced Richards's (1997) Principle of Minimal Compliance, I mentioned his observations concerning its with island constraints on *wh*-movement. If the first instance of *wh*-movement in a Bulgarian multiple question satisfies Subjacency, the Subjacency effect weakens or disappears for subsequent instances of *wh*-movement. The first instance of movement pays a "Subjacency tax" valid for the subsequent instances of movement. I repeat the relevant example, (52).

PMC improves Subjacency violations

(94) a. *Koja kniga otreče senatorăt [mălvata če iska da zabrani ____]?
        which book denied the-senator the-rumor that wanted to ban
        'Which book did the senator deny the rumor that he wanted to ban?'
     b. ?Koj senator koja kniga otreče ____ [mălvata če iska da zabrani____]?

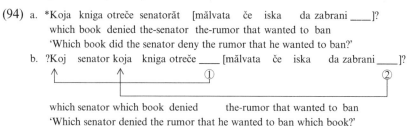

        which senator which book denied   the-rumor that wanted to ban
        'Which senator denied the rumor that he wanted to ban which book?'

The subsequent discussion of *wh*-feature movement raises the question of whether *wh*-feature movement, like overt phrasal movement in Bulgarian, pays a "Subjacency tax," just as it pays an "AC tax." The answer seems to be that it does not.

Wh-feature movement does not pay a "Subjacency tax"

(95) a. ??Which book did the senator deny the rumor that he wanted to ban?

    b. ??Which book did which senator deny the rumor that he wanted to ban?

(96) a. *What would you be upset if the reporter revealed ____ about whom?

    b. *What would who be upset if the reporter revealed ____ about whom?

(97) a. *What do you want to applaud the person that gave ____ to whom?

    b. *What does who want to applaud the person that gave ____ to whom?

One can imagine a number of reasons why *wh*-feature movement, in contrast to phrasal movement, might not pay a "Subjacency tax." For example: *wh*-feature movement is *covert*, in that pronunciation continues to target the *wh*-morpheme in its lower, original position. Quite generally, island violations do not cause deviance when the trace position receives a pronunciation. (This is how Perlmutter (1972) explained the ameliorating effect of resumptive pronouns; also see Pesetsky 1997, 1998.) Conceivably, movement that fails to "leave a gap" does not pay a "Subjacency *tax*" because it does not trigger the Subjacency *effect*. Likewise, if feature movement is really *morpheme* movement, its covert status may explain the absence of a Subjacency effect and the absence of "Subjacency tax" paying.

Another possibility is suggested by the research of Ochi (1998), developing earlier ideas by Takahashi (1994). Recall from section 1.1 that Chomsky (1995) decomposes phrasal movement into two distinct operations: Attract F (feature attraction) and "generalized pied-piping" (which forces the copying of phrasal material). Ochi (1998) argues that it is the "generalized pied-piping" component of phrasal movement that is responsible for many of the island effects often grouped under the rubric of the Subjacency Condition. He suggests that these island effects arise from a conflict between a requirement that generalized pied-piping copy a phrase to the closest possible landing site and other requirements that prevent movement from targeting these very positions. As Ochi points out, this proposal entails that pure feature movement should not show these island effects at all—to which I would now add that pure feature movement should also not pay any "tax" that allows later instances of phrasal movement to escape these island effects.[67]

As a final possibility, we might take the contrast between (94) and (95)–(97) as a sign of a deeper inaccuracy in the picture painted so far. Phrasal movement obeys both AC and Subjacency, whereas what I have called "feature movement" obeys only AC. The fact that phrasal movement obeys a superset of the conditions on "feature movement" might indicate that what I have been calling "feature movement," though it might be a subcomponent of movement, is something quite different from the operations traditionally called "movement." This is, in fact, the proposal advanced by Chomsky (1998). He suggests that phenomena he previously identified (Chomsky 1995) as instances of feature movement are actually the result of a simpler operation called *Agree*. Agree merely establishes a link between an attracting head and the features that it seeks, without the copying operation characteristic of movement. Movement itself is simply Agree plus this copying.[68]

To keep the discussion as clear and simple as possible, I will not explore further the consequences of choosing one or another variant of the feature movement proposal. What seems evident is this: there is an operation O that has certain manifest properties:

How O is like phrasal movement
1. O is feature-driven.
2. O obeys AC.
3. O interacts with phrasal movement for the purposes of the PMC as applied to AC.

How O is unlike phrasal movement
1. O does not copy and delete phrases.
2. O does not display Subjacency effects.
3. O does not interact with phrasal movement for the purposes of the PMC as applied to Subjacency effects.

Other questions about this operation cannot be answered using the facts at hand.

On the other hand, there is an entirely different set of facts that reinforces the conclusions I have already reached and the particular analysis of apparent Superiority violations I have presented. By reinforcing my conclusions with new evidence, I support the proposal I have advanced—incomplete though it may be in certain respects. I turn to this new source of evidence in the next chapter.

Chapter 5

The Intervention Effect and the Typology of Interrogative Complementizers

One of the linchpins of my hypothesis has been the idea that multiple questions are introduced by a complementizer ($C_{m\text{-spec}}$) that requires *wh*-movement to establish a multiple-specifier configuration. This property of $C_{m\text{-spec}}$ helped explain why only binary questions show the Superiority effect in English. The argument that the multiple-specifier requirement is not a deus ex machina came from Bulgarian, where failure to move at least two *wh*-phrases in a multiple question produces sharp unacceptability (except in a D-linked environment), a situation that contrasts with the mild deviance produced when additional *wh*-phrases are not fronted. Still, it would be useful to have converging evidence that the number of specifiers associated with $C_{m\text{-spec}}$ is relevant to the detection of a Superiority effect.

In this chapter I provide converging evidence of just this sort and in the process shed light on other aspects of the proposed account. In particular, I will tie up a loose end from chapter 1. In section 1.3 I noted three situations in which an otherwise expected Superiority effect is not found. I have dealt with two of them: English multiple questions with D-linking and multiple questions with more than two *wh*-phrases. I have not yet discussed the third: the case of German, where, as (34) illustrated, even binary questions fail to display a Superiority effect. More interesting still is the fact that English and German turn out to fit into a simple typology of *wh*-specifier interactions—of which Japanese exemplifies the one language type undiscussed so far (see sections 5.5 and 5.6).

The English data I will discuss are partly original to this book, but are modeled in crucial ways on German paradigms investigated by Beck (1996), whose work inspired this chapter. After considering the crucial English cases, I will turn to Beck's German discoveries.

5.1   The Intervention Effect in English Multiple Questions

In chapter 4 I examined several apparent exceptions to the Superiority effect: acceptable multiple questions with wh_1-in-situ. The impossibility of ACD in wh_1 revealed at a minimum that there is something special about wh_1 in such cases. A phenomenon first noted by É. Kiss (1986) and Hornstein (1995) shows another property of wh_1-in-situ that teaches a similar lesson. In apparent counterexamples to the Superiority effect, something special happens when a scope-taking element such as negation intervenes between wh_1 and the C_{m-spec} with which it is associated. For many speakers, at least as a first reaction, such examples are completely unacceptable. For other speakers (and perhaps for all speakers when the possibility is pointed out to them), the examples are acceptable so long as they receive a "single-pair" rather than a pair-list reading.

A representative paradigm is displayed in (98). Examples (98a) and (98b) are experimental controls—normal multiple questions in which wh_1 has undergone overt phrasal movement. Nothing special happens when negation intervenes between C_{m-spec} and wh_2-in-situ in such cases. Example (98c) shows wh_1-in-situ (i.e., an apparent Superiority violation). Here, if I am correct, the first instance of wh-movement is feature movement of *which person*. In this example negation has not moved with the auxiliary verb to C and thus remains lower than wh_1-in-situ. Once again, not surprisingly, English speakers note no special effect. Example (98d) is the example that contrasts crucially. It is identical to (98c), except that the clitic form of negation moves to C_{m-spec} with the auxiliary verb. As a consequence of this movement, negation intervenes between wh_1 and C_{m-spec}. Example (98d) does produce special judgments.

Intervention effect with not
(98) a.   Which person ____ did not read which book?
     b.   Which person ____ didn't read which book?
     c.   Which book did which person not read ____?
     d.   *Which book didn't which person read ____?
          [cf. also *Which book did which person read ____?*]

Though, as the asterisk indicates, many speakers regard (98d) as completely unacceptable, the marginal acceptability of the single-pair reading in this and similar examples will be noted by superscripting and underscoring the judgment indication. The single-pair reading for (98d) asks for the name of a single person and a single book, such that the person did not read the book. For example, suppose you pass a classroom and hear the teacher yelling. You know that this teacher only yells at the class when a student has failed to read his or her book for that day. In such a context (and only in such a context), some speakers accept a question like *Which book didn't which person read today?* For the time being I will put aside the single-pair readings of examples like these and confine my presentation of judgments on multiple questions to the pair-list reading.

Following Hagstrom's (1998) terminology, I will call the type of effect seen in (98d) an *intervention effect*. The intervention effect is less sharp when wh_1 is not a subject, but much the same judgment obtains.[69]

Intervention effect with not—*nonsubjects*
(99) a.   Which issue should I not discuss ____ with which diplomat?
     b. [??]Which diplomat should I not discuss which issue with ____?
       [cf. *Which diplomat should I discuss which issue with ____?*]

The same judgment can be produced when other negative expressions and other downward-entailing phrases intervene between wh_1 and $C_{m\text{-spec}}$, showing that elements other than clausal negation function as interveners.

Intervention effect with no one
(100) a.   Which book did no one give ____ to which student?
      b. [??]Which student did no one give which book to ____?
        [cf. *Which student did Mary give which book to ____?*]

Intervention effect with never
(101) a.   Which topic did he claim which student would never talk
        about ____?
      b. [??]Which topic did he never claim which student would talk
        about ____?
        [cf. *Which student did he never claim ____ would talk about which topic?*]

Intervention effect with very few
(102) a.   Which picture did very few children want to show ____ to
        which teacher?
      b. [??]Which teacher did very few children want to show which
        picture to ____?
        [cf. *Which teacher did she want to show which picture to ____?*]

Intervention effect with only
(103) a.   Which girl did only Mary introduce ____ to which boy?
      b. [??]Which boy did only Mary introduce which girl to ____?
        [cf. *Which girl did only Mary introduce ____ to which boy?*]

The intervention effect is not a property of "overt syntax"; instead, it cares about the scope (LF position) of the intervener. For example, in (104), which should be compared with (103), the acceptability of the pair-list reading reemerges so long as *only Mary* receives matrix scope. Some degree of focus stress on *only Mary* facilitates this reading.

Intervention effect disappears with wide scope of only
(104) Sue asked which boy only Mary introduced which girl to ____.
      [i.e., Mary is the only person such that Sue asked which boy this person introduced which girl to]

Although downward-entailing elements produce the most easily detected intervention effects, it seems that other quantifiers produce a similar effect.[70] Consider, for example, a nonmultiple question with a universal quantifier, such as (105).

Wh-*quantifier scope ambiguity*
(105) Which newspaper did everyone write to ____ about this book?

This type of question displays a well-known ambiguity (Engdahl 1980; May 1985) between a pair-list or distributive reading (for which a well-formed answer provides a list of people paired with the newspapers they wrote to) and a single-answer reading (which asks for the name of a single newspaper such that everyone wrote to it).[71] Although controversies abound concerning the syntax and semantics of the distributive reading (see, e.g., Chierchia 1993), one common and plausible conjecture derives the distributive reading from an LF representation in which the universal quantifier takes wide scope over the *wh*-expression. If we imagine that wide scope for *everyone* results from movement to a position above *which newspaper* (CP-adjunction, perhaps), the LF representation for the distributive reading of (105) is approximately (106).

LF representation for the distributive reading of (105)
(106) everyone$_x$ [which newspaper$_y$ $C_{1\text{-spec}}$ x write to y about this book]

The ambiguity survives in multiple-*wh* questions like (107).

Wh-*quantifier scope ambiguity in questions with overt movement*
(107) Which newspaper did everyone write to ____ about which book?
      [ambiguous]

On a wide-scope reading for *everyone*, (107) asks for triplet answers that, for each person picked out by *everyone*, give the newspaper and the book such that that person wrote to the newspaper about the book. That is, a possible answering pattern might be (108).

Wide-scope answering pattern
(108) Bill wrote to the *New York Times* about book X, Mary wrote to the *Boston Globe* about book Y, and Tom wrote to the *Maquoketa Sentinel* about book Z.

On a narrow-scope reading for *everyone*, (107) asks for pair-list answers of the form exemplified by (109).

Narrow-scope answering pattern
(109) Everyone wrote to the *New York Times* about book X, everyone wrote to the *Boston Globe* about book Y, and everyone wrote to the *Maquoketa Sentinel* about book Z.

Given the ambiguity of (107), the nonambiguity of (110) is striking.

Intervention effect disappears with wide scope of every
(110) Which book did everyone write to which newspaper about ____?
[unambiguous]

This example is the same as (107), except that wh_2 has undergone overt phrasal movement instead of wh_1. Consequently, *everyone* intervenes between wh_1 and $C_{\text{m-spec}}$. If all things were equal, (110) might be expected to allow the same two answering patterns as (107). Though it takes some work to see, I believe that (110) lacks the reading that would yield the narrow-scope answering pattern in (109). Unless the two *wh*-phrases are accorded a single-pair reading, a question like (110) can only be asked in expectation of an answer like (108). A single-pair reading for the two *wh*-phrases is also available in (110)—that is, a reading that invites a simple answer like *Everyone wrote to the New York Times about book X*. This is not surprising, since the intervention effect is not found with single-pair readings.[72] This fact seems to reinforce the observation that the intervention effect is a constraint on LF that examines the scope position of the intervener.

This conclusion is supported by other, related tests. An expression like clausal negation whose scope is fixed at roughly its surface position produces the unacceptability already noted when it intervenes between wh_1-in-situ and $C_{\text{m-spec}}$. There are also certain types of expressions that do allow LF scope wider than surface scope that still do not allow scope wider than *wh* within the confines of a question. Such expressions, as predicted, also produce unacceptability rather than disambiguation when inserted between wh_1-in-situ and $C_{m\text{-spec}}$. These expressions include *no one* and *only NP*, which I have already examined, as well as *almost every NP* (e.g., *almost everyone*), which contrasts minimally with *everyone*.[73] Assigning wide scope to these expressions at the outer boundary of a question seems to be impossible. This scope assignment may run afoul of something like (111), with the consequences documented in (112).[74]

Unaskable questions

(111) A clause interpreted as a question may not request anything less than a full answer.

Examples of unaskable questions

(112) a. Which newspaper did almost everyone write to ____ about this book? [*cannot be used to express the following request for information*: "Give me an almost complete list of people paired with the newspapers they wrote to about this book."]

   b. Which book did no one give ____ to John? [*cannot be used to express the following request for information*: "Don't tell me which book anyone gave to John."][75]

   c. Which teacher did very few children want to visit ____? [*cannot be used to express the following request for information*: "There are a number of children who wanted to visit a variety of teachers. Answer the question 'What teacher did he/she want to visit?' for a very small number of these children (and don't bother providing the rest of the answers)."]

   d. Which girl did only Mary introduce ____ to John? [*cannot be used to express the following request for information*: "I know that several people introduced girls to John. Tell me which girl Mary introduced to him, but don't tell me which girls other people introduced to him."]

Since the only way around the intervention effect in examples like (100b) and (103b) involves wide scope for the intervener that violates (111), the examples cannot be saved. The same explanation accounts for the contrast between (110) with *every* and a comparable example with *almost every*.

Intervention effect with almost every

(113) ^{??}Which book did almost everyone write to which newspaper about ____?

As predicted, it is difficult or impossible to understand (113) as any sort of pair-list multiple question. To the extent that it is acceptable at all, it is only a request for a single-pair answer (e.g., *Almost everyone wrote to this newspaper about that book*).

Quantifier float provides a similar demonstration. Floated quantifiers are restricted in scope to their surface position. For example, whereas (114a) has a reading in which *each student* has wider scope than *at least one teacher*, (114b) does not.

Frozen scope with quantifier float

(114) a. At least one teacher made each student sing the national anthem.

b. At least one teacher made the students each sing the national anthem.

The same observation holds for the relative scope of *each* and *wh*. Whereas (115a) may be a request for an answer that provides adult-kid-book triplets, (115b) is at best a request for adult-book pairs, such that each kid in the group will persuade the adult to read the book.[76]

Frozen scope with quantifier float in multiple questions

(115) a. Tell me which adult each kid will try to persuade ____ to read which book.

b. Tell me which adult the kids will each try to persuade ____ to read which book.

If we now alter these examples by overtly fronting wh_2 (*which book*) rather than wh_1, the impossibility of wide scope when *each* is floated should produce an intervention effect from which the only (marginal) escape is the single-pair reading. This seems correct.

Intervention effect with quantifier float

(116) a. Tell me which book each kid will try to persuade which adult to read ____.

b. ??Tell me which book the kids will each try to persuade which adult to read ____.

The paradigms I have discussed so far seem to support the following (interim) characterization of the intervention effect as it shows up in English:

Intervention effect in English

(117) A scope-bearing element (especially quantifiers and negation) may not intervene at LF between wh_1-in-situ and the $C_{m\text{-spec}}$ with which it is associated.

The data presented to support this characterization come from instances of wh_1-in-situ in binary questions with D-linking. Our other case of wh_1-in-situ—questions with more than two wh-phrases—appears to show the same pattern of intervention effects. This is particularly evident when negation is the intervener. Taking as baseline a triple-wh question without negation, but with wh_1-in-situ, we can easily see that negation intervening between wh_1 and $C_{m\text{-}spec}$ (as in (118b) and (119b)) has an effect not found when negation is lower than wh_1 (as in (118a) and (119a)). The effect is the familiar one: the example is either unacceptable or else acceptable with only a single-pair reading.

Intervention effect with not *in nonbinary, non-D-linked multiple questions*
(118) *Baseline:* What did who give ____ to whom?
    a.   What did who not give ____ to whom?
    b.   *What didn't who give ____ to whom?

(119) *Baseline:* What did Bill persuade who to give ____ to whom?
    a.   What did Bill persuade who not to give ____ to whom?
    b.   ^{??}What did Bill not persuade who to give ____ to whom?

The other interveners discussed above seem to behave similarly. Because questions that include three wh-phrases plus a quantifier are complex, judgments on these examples do not come easily. Thoughtful consideration is necessary.

Intervention effect with no one *in nonbinary, non-D-linked multiple questions*
(120) a.   What did who say no one gave ____ to whom?
    b.   ^{??}What did no one say who gave ____ to whom?

Intervention effect with never *in nonbinary, non-D-linked multiple questions*
(121) a.   What did he claim who would never talk about ____ with whom?
    b.   ^{??}What topic did he never claim who would talk about ____ with whom?

Intervention effect with very few *in nonbinary, non-D-linked multiple questions*
(122) a.   Who did very few people persuade ____ to give what to whom for Christmas?
    b.   ^{??}What did very few people persuade who to give ____ to whom for Christmas?

Intervention effect with only *in nonbinary, non-D-linked multiple questions*
(123) a.   What did who persuade only Mary to buy ____ where?
      b. $^{??}$What did only Mary persuade whom to buy ____ where?

5.2   The Intervention Effect in German Separation Constructions

The intervention effect in English is particularly interesting because it singles out wh_1-in-situ. As (118a) and (119a) show, no intervention effect is observed with other *wh*-phrases—even in questions that display wh_1-in-situ. Since we do not know for sure whether there is an overall preference for phrasal movement or for feature movement, the one English *wh*-phrase that we can be certain has undergone feature movement is wh_1-in-situ in apparent counterexamples to Superiority. Consequently, it is tempting to see the intervention effect as a diagnostic for some property that distinguishes *wh*-feature movement from phrasal *wh*-movement of the sort we have been examining.[77]

One property that distinguishes *wh*-feature movement from *wh*-phrase movement in English is the fact that feature movement leaves the restriction on *wh*-quantification inside the clause, whereas phrasal movement typically pied-pipes the restriction with the *wh*-phrase. It could be that "separation" of the sort seen in *wh*-feature movement is the cause of the intervention effect.[78]

Intervention effect (universal characterization)
(124) A semantic restriction on a quantifier (including *wh*) may not be separated from that quantifier by a scope-bearing element.

German provides interesting support for this view—support that will ultimately provide evidence for several aspects of my overall account. My discussion of German is a reworking of data and discussion from Beck 1996. I have added to Beck's paradigms in several cases and have truncated the presentation of data in others, but my debt to her work should be clear throughout. I will not take a stand on the question of *why* a constraint like (124) should hold, instead limiting my discussion to the truth of the generalization itself and its role in supporting the proposals about *wh*-movement presented here. For a view of intervention effects quite similar to (124), and a possible account, see Honcoop 1998, esp. 19, 81ff.

German displays several constructions in which phrasal *wh*-movement raises a portion of an argument phrase overtly, leaving the remainder behind in the clause. We can call this family of constructions *separation*. Among the phrases that can separate in this manner are phrases of the form "*wh*-word + partitive-PP," "*wh*-word + adjective," and "*wh*-word + *all*." I will leave open the exact nature of *wh*-separation. It might involve an internal structure for the phrases in question that simply permits a subconstituent to count as a *wh*-phrase and extract accordingly. Alternatively, it might involve scrambling of an expression that is to be stranded out of its *wh*-phrase, with phrasal *wh*-movement of the remnant. Either way, it is a construction that strands—inside its clause—material belonging to the restriction of a *wh*-phrase. Strikingly, the construction is subject to the intervention effect, as the paradigms in (125)–(126) make clear.

Who + among DP

(125) a. *No separation, no intervener*
      [Wen   von den Musikern] hat Hans ____ getroffen?
      whom of   the musicians has Hans   met
      'Who among the musicians has Hans met?'

    b. *Separation, no intervener*
      Wen hat Hans [____ von den Musikern] getroffen?

    c. *No separation, intervener*
      [Wen   von den Musikern] hat keine Studentin getroffen?
      whom of   the musicians has no   student   met
      'Who among the musicians has no student met?'

    d. *Separation, intervener*
      ??Wen hat keine Studentin [____ von den Musikern] getroffen?

Who + all

(126) a. *No separation, no intervener*
      [Wen   alles] hat Hans ____ gesehen?
      whom all   has Hans   seen
      'Who all did Hans see?'

    b. *Separation, no intervener*
      Wen hat Hans [____ alles] gesehen?

    c. *No separation, intervener*
      [Wen   alles] hat niemand ____ gesehen?
      whom all   has no-one   seen
      'Who all did no one see?'

    d. *Separation, intervener*
      ??Wen hat niemand [____ alles] gesehen?

What + adjective
(127) [no separation impossible, for unknown reasons]
      b. *Separation, no intervener*
          Was hat Gretchen heute [____ schönes] gemacht?
          what has Gretchen today   nice   done
          'What nice thing did Gretchen do today?'
      d. *Separation, intervener*
          ^{??}Was hat niemand heute [____ schönes] gemacht?
           what has no-one   today   nice   done
          'What nice thing did no one do today?'

Other facets of our discussion of English can be reproduced here as well. For example, (128) has only a distributive reading.

Distributive reading only
(128) Wen   hat jeder   ____ alles gesehen?
      whom has everyone   all   seen
      'Who all did everyone see?'

    The common behavior of German separation constructions and English wh_1-in-situ supports my hypotheses nicely.[79] If English wh_1-in-situ involves feature or morpheme movement (as argued above), it is actually simply an instance of "separation": a piece of the *wh*-phrase—in this case just the *wh*-morpheme or feature—moves to the complementizer, stranding the restriction inside its clause. If we adopt the alternative that posits an agreement operation in these cases, we still see a separation of the interrogative C-system from the restriction of a *wh*-phrase. Consequently, even if this variant of my views on English wh_1-in-situ is correct, these constructions should share the intervention effect with the more obvious instances of separation found in German.[80]

    In fact, one dialect of English actually displays a German-like separation construction that seems to show the intervention effect. As described by McCloskey (2000), the West Ulster dialect of Irish English shares with many colloquial registers a series of *wh*-phrases modified by *all*: *who all*, *what all*, and so on. The semantic effect of the morpheme *all* is roughly to presuppose that the answer will be a plurality. The West Ulster dialect, unlike others, allows *all* to be separated from its *wh*-phrase.

West Ulster what all *separation*
(129) a. What all did Mary get on her birthday?
      b. What did Mary get ____ all on her birthday?

When this occurs, an intervention effect seems to arise.[81]

West Ulster intervention effect with separation
(130) a ??What did Mary not buy ____ all up the town?
     b. *What did only Mary get ____ all on her birthday?
     c. What did everybody get ____ all on Christmas morning?
        [distributive reading only]
     d. *What did almost everybody get ____ all on Christmas
        morning?
     e. *What did very few people get ____ all for Christmas?

The observation must be treated with some caution, since even the "unseparated" variants of (130) are felt by speakers to be strange (e.g., *?What all did Mary not buy up the town?*). Nonetheless, the separated versions are said to be detectably worse.

In any case, if I am right about the unity of the intervention effect in English multiple questions and German separation constructions, then we must accept a characterization like (124) instead of the one offered by Beck (1996). According to Beck, the intervention effect in German separation constructions is an island condition on traces formed by covert phrasal movement—in particular, a condition on a rule that moves the restriction to its quantifier in separation constructions. (A similar formulation is given by Hasegawa (1994), who treats it as an LF-particular case of the Minimal Link Condition.) In Beck's (1996, 39) formulation, *quantifier-induced barriers* cannot be crossed by traces that are created solely "at LF" (i.e., by covert phrasal movement).

Beck's proposals
(131) a. *Quantifier-induced barrier*
        The first node that dominates a quantifier, its restriction, and
        its nuclear scope is a quantifier-induced barrier.
     b. *Minimal Quantified Structure Constraint*
        If an LF trace β is dominated by a quantifier-induced barrier,
        α, then the binder of β must also be dominated by α.

The earlier discussion of ACD revealed that the stranded material in English *wh*-feature movement does *not* undergo covert phrasal movement of any sort. Consequently, if the intervention effect in German separation constructions is the same phenomenon we have examined in English, the Minimal Quantified Structure Constraint as stated in (131b) is probably incorrect. Instead, something like (124) must be true.[82]

5.3 The Intervention Effect in German Multiple Questions

If the intervention effect diagnoses the presence of "restriction material" stranded within an interrogative clause, it can be used as a probe to discover instances of feature movement in languages and constructions where the previous test, ACD, is unavailable. German, for example, lacks VP-ellipsis and seems to lack other instances of anaphora with the right set of properties.[83] If we use the intervention effect as a probe for feature movement in German multiple questions, we discover a notable difference between English and German. I will argue that a partial explanation for this difference is available, and that this explanation in turn supports the overall architecture of my proposals.

In German, unlike in English, the intervention effect in multiple questions is not limited to cases of wh_1-in-situ. Instead, *no wh*-in-situ may be separated from C by the sorts of elements that produce the intervention effect.[84] (I will not prejudge the nature of the complementizer by calling it $C_{m\text{-}spec}$, for reasons that will become clear shortly.) Example (132), for instance, is a multiple question in which nominative wh_1-in-situ has undergone overt phrasal *wh*-movement and accusative wh_2 has not. When the dative NP that intervenes between wh_2 and its C is an ordinary NP like *dem Karl*, the result is fully acceptable. When the intervener is a negative quantifier, as in (133b), the result is unacceptable in a quite familiar way. The result is unacceptable unless (for some speakers) a single-pair answer is expected.[85] That this is an "intervention" effect is made clear by the contrast between (133a) and (133b). These examples differ only in that the accusative *wh*-phrase appears to the left of the dative in (133a), presumably as a consequence of scrambling.

Baseline: no intervener, no intervention effect
(132) Welche Kinder   haben ___ dem Karl   welche Bilder   zeigen wollen?
       which children-NOM have   the Karl-DAT which pictures-ACC show   wanted
       'Which children wanted to show Karl which pictures?'

Intervention effect (German) with no one
(133)
a. Welche Kinder   haben welche Bilder   niemandem zeigen wollen? [scrambling of ACC]
    which children-NOM have   which pictures-ACC no-one-DAT show   wanted
    'Which children wanted to show nobody which pictures?'
b. ??Welche Kinder haben niemandem welche Bilder zeigen wollen?

The set of interveners that produce the effect appears to be the set now familiar to us. Although I have not displayed the relevant examples, scrambling the accusative wh_2 over the dative NP eliminates the intervention effect. Examples (134)–(135) display downward-entailing interveners.

Intervention effect (German) with very few

(134) [22]Welche Kinder   haben sehr wenigen Lehrern welche Bilder   zeigen wollen?
      which children-NOM have   very few teachers-DAT which pictures-ACC show   wanted
      'Which children wanted to show very few teachers which pictures?'

Intervention effect (German) with only

(135) [22]Wer   hat nur dem Karl   welche Bücher   gegeben?
      who-NOM has only the Karl-DAT which books-ACC given
      'Who gave only Karl which books?'

Intervention by *jeder* 'everyone' is possible, so long as *jeder* is assigned wide scope.

Intervention effect (German) with everyone

(136) Wen   hat jeder   wo   gesehen?   (wide scope for *jeder*
      whom has everyone where seen   'everyone' or single-pair
      'Who did everyone see where?'   narrow scope; otherwise
                                                "??")

Since wide scope is impossible for *fast jeder* 'almost everyone', there is no reading (except perhaps the single-pair reading) that bypasses the intervention effect.

Intervention effect (German) with almost everyone

(137) [22]Wen   hat fast   jeder   wo   gesehen?
      whom has almost everyone where seen
      'Who did almost everyone see where?'

The question to be answered here concerns the stark difference in the types of *wh*-in-situ subject to the effect. Why is only wh_1-in-situ subject to the effect in English, whereas all *wh*-in-situ are subject to it in German? If I am right about the character of the intervention effect, the answer must be this:

Movement in German multiple questions

(138) In a German multiple question, all *wh*-in-situ undergo *wh*-feature movement.

German multiple questions behave like separation constructions because, in a sense, they *are* separation constructions.[86]

What property of German is responsible for (138)? In particular, what distinguishes German from Bulgarian and English, which allow multiple *wh*-phrase movement? Though one might try to account for this distinction in a number of ways,[87] I will explore the possibility that it arises from differences in the inventory of complementizers available to the two types of languages.

If my proposals are correct, multiple questions in English and Bulgarian boast a special complementizer that I have called $C_{m\text{-spec}}$. As discussed, this complementizer has a *wh*-feature that can and must be deleted after attracting more than one instance of a corresponding *wh*-feature to it, either by means of phrasal movement or by means of feature movement. $C_{m\text{-spec}}$ also has a specific syntactic requirement: it must be associated with more than one specifier. This fact was visible in the patterns of overt *wh*-phrase movement in Bulgarian exemplified earlier, and it formed an important component of my explanation for the Superiority effect in English.

$C_{m\text{-spec}}$ obviously differs from the complementizer found in single-*wh* questions, since these questions cannot satisfy a multiple-specifier requirement—at least not through *wh*-movement. For this reason, I have suggested that single-*wh* questions are introduced by a complementizer that requires a single specifier: $C_{1\text{-spec}}$. The requirements of the two complementizers, first stated in (36) and (38), are repeated here. I omit, for now, the special case of D-linked questions.

Single-specifier requirement of $C_{1\text{-spec}}$
(139) $C_{1\text{-spec}}$ requires one *wh*-specifier.

Multiple-specifier requirement of $C_{m\text{-spec}}$
(140) $C_{m\text{-spec}}$ requires more than one *wh*-specifier.

Recall that both complementizers are taken to bear an uninterpretable feature, in something of Chomsky's (1995) sense. It is this feature that triggers the rule Attract, which leads to *wh*-movement.

In English and Bulgarian a question is apparently always introduced by the interrogative complementizer with the greatest "specifier potential" consistent with the instances of the *wh*-morpheme or feature that it can attract. Consequently, a question containing only one instance of the *wh*-feature is introduced by $C_{1\text{-spec}}$, but a question containing two or more instances of the *wh*-feature must be introduced by $C_{m\text{-spec}}$. Otherwise, we would not detect the Superiority effect in cases of wh_1-in-situ within binary sentences. As discussed earlier, the D-linking exception is either an exception to (140) or an exception to the rule of complementizer choice.

Suppose the rule of complementizer choice (informally stated in (141)) is universal.[88]

Complementizer Choice Rule
(141) Use the complementizer with the maximum satisfiable specifier potential.[89]

Let me now advance the hypothesis that the availability of a particular complementizer depends on the resources of the lexicon in a particular language. If this hypothesis is correct, the special facts of German *wh*-questions must be indicating that the German lexicon contains $C_{1\text{-spec}}$, but lacks $C_{m\text{-spec}}$. Because the lexicon contains $C_{1\text{-spec}}$, German *wh*-questions show one instance of phrasal *wh*-movement, which is overt, as in English. Because the lexicon lacks $C_{m\text{-spec}}$, any other instance of *wh*-movement in a multiple question must involve feature movement.

If the intervention effect found with pair-list multiple questions in German is due to the separation of the *wh*-feature from the restriction, it must be the case that the pair-list reading depends on *wh*-movement. That is, something like (142) must be true, presumably as a consequence of mechanisms of semantic interpretation that I will not explore here.

Syntax of the pair-list reading for multiple questions
(142) A *wh*-expression participates in a pair-list reading within an interrogative clause only if its *wh*-feature has been attracted to the complementizer of the clause.

In English (142) can be satisfied by multiple phrasal *wh*-movement, which does not involve separation of the *wh*-feature from its restriction. Consequently, English multiple questions do not have to show an intervention effect when a *wh*-in-situ is separated from the complementizer by a scope-bearing element (except when feature movement has in fact taken place, as in apparent Superiority violations). Since German *wh*-in-situ has only feature movement at its disposal as a means of satisfying (142), pair-list readings for multiple questions always produce an intervention effect when a scope-bearing element intervenes between *wh*-in-situ and the complementizer. On this view a single-pair reading results from the failure of a *wh*-feature to undergo *wh*-movement, which in turn accounts for the lack of intervention effects with this reading.

The notion of specifier potential, though implicit in the work on multiple specifiers initiated by Ura (1996), is novel, as is the idea that questions pick the complementizer with the greatest potential. It is therefore useful (just as it was when I first introduced $C_{m\text{-}spec}$) to show that these ideas are not *dei ex machinis*, by showing that they play a role in explaining other phenomena. In the present case the Superiority effect furnishes such a demonstration.

The fact that English binary questions show a Superiority effect follows from the fact (now a consequence of (141)) that such questions involve $C_{m\text{-}spec}$—the interrogative complementizer that requires at least two specifiers. It is this fact that ruled out the spurious derivation of *What did who buy?* in (77), repeated here.

Spurious derivation of an apparent exception to Superiority (English)
(143) a. *Structure before movement*
$C_{m\text{-}spec}$ [who bought what]
b. *Step 1*
$C_{m\text{-}spec}$ attracts the *wh*-feature of *who*
F_i-C [F_i-who bought what]
c. *Step 2*
$C_{m\text{-}spec}$ attracts the *wh*-phrase *what*
what F_i-C [F_i-who bought ____]
d. *Pronounced result*
*What did who buy?

If $C_{m\text{-}spec}$ could be replaced with $C_{1\text{-}spec}$ in English, the derivation would succeed—but that would run afoul of the Complementizer Choice Rule, which requires the multiple question to be introduced by $C_{m\text{-}spec}$. On the other hand, $C_{1\text{-}spec}$ is exactly what German must use, if my proposals are correct. Consequently, German should show no Superiority effect in such examples. Derivation (144) should be just as possible as (145).

An apparent exception to Superiority: not spurious (German)
(144) a. *Structure before movement*
$C_{1\text{-}spec}$ [wer sah was]
who saw what
b. *Step 1*
$C_{1\text{-}spec}$ attracts the *wh*-feature of *wer*
F_i-$C_{1\text{-}spec}$ [F_i-wer sah was]
c. *Step 2*
$C_{1\text{-}spec}$ attracts the *wh*-phrase *was*
was F_i-$C_{1\text{-}spec}$ [F_i-wer sah]
d. *Pronounced result*
Was sah wer?

No apparent Superiority violation (German)

(145) a. *Structure before movement*

$C_{1\text{-spec}}$ [wer sah was]
                who saw what

   b. *Step 1*

$C_{1\text{-spec}}$ attracts the *wh*-phrase *wer*
wer $C_{1\text{-spec}}$ [____ sah was]

   c. *Step 2*

$C_{1\text{-spec}}$ attracts the *wh*-feature of *was*
wer F_j-$C_{1\text{-spec}}$ [____ sah F_j-was]

   d. *Pronounced result*

Wer sah was?

In fact, as has been well known since at least Haider 1986, 114, both outputs are acceptable. German speakers sometimes feel that (144) is "more natural" than (145), but I have never encountered a German speaker who felt that (144) was deviant; nor do these examples require D-linking (but see Wiltschko 1997 and Grohmann 1998 for alternative views).[90] Both outputs have a pair-list interpretation.

As Grohmann (1998) notes, the absence of the Superiority effect in German is not limited to cases in which wh_1 is a subject. Cases in which it is an object also fail to show the effect. ((146) is Grohmann's (30).)

Apparent Superiority violation: wh_1 *as object*

(146) a. Wen   hast du   überredet was zu kaufen?
         whom-ACC have you persuaded what to buy
         'Who did you persuade to buy what?'

   b. Was hast du wen überredet zu kaufen?

I take these examples to show that German generally lacks the Superiority effect.[91] This is an interesting result, since it is not otherwise obvious (independent of my proposals) why German should show greater freedom than English with respect to Superiority, but less freedom than English with respect to the intervention effect. My proposals link these two facts.[92]

Before proceeding further, I need to note that the status of Superiority effects in German is controversial. A number of investigators, including Büring (1994) and Fanselow (1991, 1997), have pointed out that long-distance *wh*-movement shows contrasts that look like a Superiority effect. (The examples in (147) are from Fanselow 1997.)

A Superiority effect with long-distance wh-*movement?*

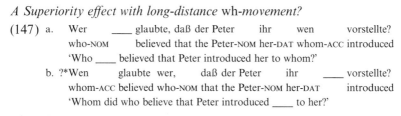

(147) a.   Wer   ____   glaubte, daß der Peter   ihr   wen   vorstellte?
         who-NOM   believed that the Peter-NOM her-DAT whom-ACC introduced
         'Who ____ believed that Peter introduced her to whom?'

      b. ?*Wen   glaubte wer,   daß der Peter   ihr   ____ vorstellte?
         whom-ACC believed who-NOM that the Peter-NOM her-DAT   introduced
         'Whom did who believe that Peter introduced ____ to her?'

One way of explaining the contrast in (147), considered by Fanselow, relies on the idea that the Superiority effect is active in German just as it is in English—the opposite of my conclusion. In this proposal what allows apparent Superiority violations in German is the possibility of scrambling. In a multiple question in which the object undergoes overt wh-movement, whereas the subject remains in situ, the object (on this view) first scrambles to a position higher than the subject. The object is now structurally higher than the subject, and consequently not only can but must be the first wh-element attracted by the interrogative complementizer.

The scrambling proposal (not adopted here)

(148) a. *Structure before movement*

         C [wer sah was]
            who saw what

     b. *Step 1*

        was scrambles to a position higher than *were*
        C [was [wer sah t$_{scrambling}$]]

     c. *Step 2*

        C attracts the wh-phrase *was*, since it is closer than *wer*
        wer C [____ [wer sah t$_{scrambling}$]]

     d. *Pronounced result*

        Was sah wer?

In order to overcome the Superiority effect in (147) in the same fashion, the embedded object would have to scramble out of the embedded finite clause in order to land in a position higher than the matrix subject. As an independent fact about German, scrambling from finite clauses is forbidden. ((149) is from Fanselow 1997.)

No scrambling from finite clauses

(149)

*... daß der Fritz   den Josef$_i$ glaubte, daß der Peter   ihr   ____$_i$ vorstellte.
      that the Fritz-NOM the Josef-ACC   believed that the Peter-NOM her-DAT   introduced
  '... that Fritz believed that Peter introduced Josef ⟨scrambled⟩ to her.'

Consequently, (147b) could only show *wh*-movement directly from the embedded clause. Since the matrix subject is closer to the interrogative complementizer, *wh*-movement from the embedded clause, at least as the first instance of *wh*-movement, is forbidden by AC.

This is an attractive competitor to my proposal, since (like my proposal) it reduces the difference in Superiority effects between German and English to an independent difference: here, the availability of scrambling in German and its unavailability in English. There is an alternative explanation for the contrast in (147), however, that does not rely on facts about scrambling. Example (147b) shows an instance of overt *wh*-movement from an embedded finite clause; (147a) does not. As it happens, many speakers reject *wh*-movement from embedded finite clauses altogether. Even the many speakers who do not reject *wh*-movement from embedded finite clauses find such examples more difficult to accept than more local instances of *wh*-movement. This factor alone could explain the contrast between (147a) and (147b).[93]

Still, if a *wh*-phrase may scramble before undergoing *wh*-movement, and if this scrambling operation allows objects to count as closer to the complementizer than subjects, we do have a source for apparent Superiority violations independent of the hypotheses presented here. Indeed, it is not established that scrambling to the left of the subject *can* feed overt *wh*-movement as the scrambling proposal assumes. For one thing, it seems to be impossible to scramble a *wh*-phrase when that phrase does not undergo subsequent overt phrasal *wh*-movement, as several researchers have noted. Fanselow (1990), for example, observes that although scrambling of a non-*wh*-phrase is acceptable inside a multiple question (as seen in (150b)), scrambling of the *wh*-phrase that does not undergo overt phrasal *wh*-movement is impossible (as seen in (150d)). (This generalization is due to Engel (1972), according to Sauerland (1998a); see also Müller and Sternefeld 1993, 483.) Example (150a) shows that Superiority is not what is at stake in (150), and (150c) is the variant of (150d) without scrambling. ((150a–d) are from Fanselow 1990, 114.) The examples in (151) provide a similar paradigm from Grewendorf and Sternefeld 1990, 5.[94]

No scrambling of wh-*in-situ*

(150) a. Wie hat wer gestern   das Auto repariert?
           how has who yesterday the car   fixed
           'How did who fix the car yesterday?'[95]

b. Wie hat das Auto gestern   wer repariert?
   how has the car   yesterday who fixed
   'How did who fix the car yesterday?'

c. Wie hat der Mann gestern   was repariert?
   how has the man   yesterday what fixed
   'How did the man yesterday fix what?'

d. *Wie hat was der Mann gestern   repariert?
   how has what the man   yesterday fixed
   'How did the man yesterday fix what?'

(151) a. Was hat wer   dem Studenten ausgeliehen?
        what has who-NOM the student-DAT lent
        'What did who lend to the student?'

b. Was hat der Professor   wem   ausgeliehen?
   what has the professor-NOM whom-DAT lent
   'What did the professor lend to whom?'

c. Wem   hat der Professor   was ausgeliehen?
   whom-DAT has the professor-NOM what lent
   'To whom did the professor lend what?'

d. ??Was hat wem   der Professor   ausgeliehen?
   what has whom-DAT the professor-NOM lent
   'What did the professor lend to whom?'

Furthermore, if separation constructions provide reliable markers of positions that *wh*-movement passes through, there are other arguments that scrambling to the left of the subject cannot feed *wh*-movement. One argument was pointed out to me by Günther Grewendorf (personal communication). In (125) we examined a separation construction in which a *wh*-word like *wer/wen* 'who' is separated from a restrictor like *von den Musikern* 'of the musicians', stranding the restrictor in object position. Such separation is possible in derived positions as well. (152a), for example, shows *von den Musikern* 'of the musicians' stranded in a [Spec, CP] through which a *wh*-phrase has passed. (The presence of overt material in [Spec, CP] correlates with "verb-second" (movement of V to C) and with the absence of the complementizer *daß*, as discussed by Den Besten (1983).) The possibility of "separation" in [Spec, CP] contrasts sharply with the impossibility of a comparable separation in a post-complementizer scrambling position, seen in (152c), which contrasts minimally with the unscrambled (152b).

No separation in scrambled position
(152)

a. *Separation in [Spec, CP]*
   ?Wen glaubst du [___ von den Musikern] hat Hans gesehen?
   whom believe you   of the musicians has Hans seen
   'Who among the musicians do you believe that Hans saw?'
b. *Separation in object position*
   Ich weiß nicht, wen du glaubst, daß Hans [___ von den Musikern] gesehen hat.
   I know not whom you believe that Hans   of the musicians seen has
   'I don't know who among the musicians you believe that Hans saw.'
c. *Separation in scrambled position*
   *Ich weiß nicht, wen du glaubst, daß [___ von den Musikern] Hans gesehen hat.
   I know not whom you believe that   of the musicians Hans seen has
   'I don't know who among the musicians you believe that Hans saw.'

Similar paradigms can be constructed with other separation constructions, except that separation across a finite-clause boundary seems degraded in the first place in some of these cases, and separation in [Spec, CP] is not possible.[96]

*No separation in scrambled position (*was alles*)*

(153) a. *Separation in [Spec, CP]*
   *Wen glaubst du [___ alles] hat Hans eingeladen?
   whom believe you   all has Hans invited
   b. *Separation in object position*
   %Ich weiß nicht, wen du glaubst, daß Hans [___ alles] eingeladen hat.
   I know not whom you believe that Hans   all invited has
   'I don't know who-all you believe that Hans invited.'
   c. *Separation in scrambled position*
   *Ich weiß nicht, wen du glaubst, daß [___ alles] Hans eingeladen hat.
   I know not whom you believe that   all Hans invited has
   'I don't know who-all you believe that Hans invited.'

There might, of course, be some special explanation for the failure of separation in the scrambled position. I suggest instead that (152) and (153) illustrate the same point as (150) and (151): that *wh*-phrases are simply not scrambled to the left of the subject in the first place.

5.4 Further Discussion of Fanselow's Proposal

Fanselow (1997) provides two arguments in favor of the scrambling proposal that need to be considered. Since this section does not contribute to the forward flow of argumentation, it can be viewed as an appendix to the preceding section and can be skipped without losing the thread. None-

theless, Fanselow's arguments are an important challenge to this portion
of our ideas about *wh*-movement, and they merit discussion.

5.4.1   Argument 1

Suppose certain separation constructions actually involve, not direct *wh*-
movement of a portion of the bigger phrase that might have moved, but
scrambling of the phrase ultimately left behind, followed by *wh*-movement
of the remnant that includes the trace of scrambling.

Separation via scrambling

(154) a. *Starting point*

C ... X [wieviel   Bücher über   Hans] ...
                how-many books about Hans

    b. *Step 1*

über Hans scrambles to the left of X

C ... über Hans$_i$ X [wieviel Bücher t_i] ...

    c. *Step 2*

The remnant *wh*-phrase undergoes phrasal *wh*-movement

[wieviel Bücher t_i] C ... über Hans$_i$ X ...

Müller (1996) and Müller and Sternefeld (1993) have observed that a
constituent from which scrambling has taken place may not itself undergo
scrambling. If this is the case, then the *wh*-phrase cannot itself undergo
scrambling as a precursor to *wh*-movement. Now consider a situation in
which *über Hans* is replaced by a *wh*-phrase such as *über wen* 'about
whom' in the starting point of (154). If *über wen* undergoes scrambling,
then, by Müller's generalization, the remnant [*wieviel Bücher t*] may not
itself undergo scrambling. If Superiority holds in German as it does in
English, we expect the (now) higher *wh*-phrase *über wen* to be the only
phrase attractable by the interrogative complementizer. This prediction is
borne out.[97]

A Superiority effect in German?

(155)

a. Ich wüßte gerne, über wen$_i$ er [wieviel   Bücher t$_i$] gleichzeitig   kritisieren kann.
    I   knew eagerly about whom he how-many books   simultaneously criticize   can
    'I would like to know how many books about whom he can simultaneously criticize.'

b. ?*Ich wüßte gerne, [wieviel Bücher t$_i$] er gleichzeitig über wen$_i$ kritisieren kann. [same
    example with *über Hans* replacing *über wen* is fine]

Notice, however, that (155b) differs from (155a) in other ways that we
know influence acceptability. For one thing, (155b) is a Weak Crossover

configuration: the variable associated with *wen* is an argument of [*wieviel Bücher t*], which c-commands *wen*. The Weak Crossover effect may be particularly strong with *wh*-feature movement (an observation also made, in slightly different terms, by Miyagawa (1998)).[98] This fact alone might produce the judgment given, which would be (in my approach) akin to the effects seen in English examples like (156) and (157b).[99]

Weak Crossover effects induced by wh-*feature movement*
(156) ??[How many books about him$_i$] did who$_i$ show ____ to whom?

(157) a.   Which of his friends ____ ordered which boy to congratulate
            Sue ____?
      b. [*]Which of his friends did Sue order which boy to
            congratulate ____?

5.4.2   Argument 2

If separation constructions arise from a derivation like (154), then the "separated" piece of the *wh*-moved phrase is "an indicator of the uppermost position the *wh* phrase had prior to *wh*-attraction" (Fanselow 1997), since, by Müller's generalization, the *wh*-phrase could not have scrambled before undergoing *wh*-movement. Therefore, if another *wh*-phrase is found higher than the separated piece, and the Superiority effect holds in German just as it does in English, it should be that higher *wh*-phrase that needs to undergo overt *wh*-movement.

Thus, for example, in (158a) the underscored phrase *von den Studenten* 'of the students' marks the highest position that the remnant [*wen t*] could have occupied before *wh*-movement. Consequently, when the subject *der Peter* in (158a) is replaced by the *wh*-phrase *wer* 'who' in (158b), the result is a Superiority violation (from Fanselow's perspective), since *wer*—as the higher *wh*-expression—should have undergone overt *wh*-movement instead of [*wen t*]. In (158c) scrambling of *wen von den Studenten* took place before *von den Studenten* scrambled further. Since the launching site for *wh*-movement of [*wen t*] is higher than the subject *wh*-phrase *wer* in this example, it is [*wen t*] that undergoes overt *wh*-movement, with no problem.

A Superiority effect in German when remnant movement controls for scrambling?
(158)

a.   [Wen t$_i$] hat denn der Peter im   Sommersemester von den Studenten$_i$ prüfen   wollen?
      whom   has PRT the Peter in-the summer-term   of the students   examine wanted
      'Who among the students did Peter want to examine in the summer term?'

b. ?*[Wen t$_i$] hat denn *wer* im Sommersemester <u>von den Studenten</u>$_i$ prüfen wollen?

c. [Wen t$_i$] hat denn <u>von den Studenten</u>$_i$ *wer* im Sommersemester prüfen wollen?

Here too there is an immediate alternative explanation. Example (158b) is ruled out by the intervention effect, since the scope-bearing element *wer* intervenes between a part of the restriction on *wen* and *wen* itself. As Günther Grewendorf (personal communication) points out, *wh*-phrases in situ count as interveners for the intervention effect.

An alternative explanation for (158): an intervention effect induced by wh-*in-situ*

(159) a.   Was hat der Professor dem Studenten [_____ alles] geraten?
            what has the professor the student-DAT   all   advised
            'What-all did the professor advise the student?'

    b. *Was hat wer dem Studenten [_____ alles] geraten?
            what has who the student-DAT   all   advised
            'What-all did who advise the student?'

I now return to the main line of discussion.

5.5   Japanese and a Typology of *Wh*-Specifiers

Sections 5.1–5.3 provided support for a key component of my account of apparent Superiority violations: the notion of specifier potential. According to my proposal, the German lexicon contains only $C_{1\text{-spec}}$, whereas the English (and Bulgarian) lexicon contains both $C_{1\text{-spec}}$ and $C_{m\text{-spec}}$. This lexical difference, I have argued, is the key to gross differences in the distribution of the intervention effect in German and English multiple questions. Since German allows only one *wh*-specifier per question, the restrictions of the other *wh*-phrases in a multiple question remain separated from the interrogative complementizer. This generates an intervention effect when a scope-bearing element occupies an intervening position. Since English allows multiple *wh*-specifiers, the intervention effect is found only in cases where an apparent Superiority violation indicates that feature movement has taken place from a *wh*-phrase in situ.

Alongside interrogative complementizers that require multiple specifiers and interrogative complementizers that require a single specifier, it is reasonable to expect to find an interrogative complementizer that tolerates no specifiers whatsoever: that is, $C_{0\text{-spec}}$. As it happens, my hypotheses make very specific predictions about the properties of questions introduced by $C_{0\text{-spec}}$. I will argue that $C_{0\text{-spec}}$ does exist and that these predictions seem to be fully confirmed. In particular, I will suggest that

Japanese (and Korean) *wh*-questions are introduced by $C_{0\text{-spec}}$. Japanese/
Korean, German, and English/Bulgarian thus round out the paradigm of
specifier potential for interrogative complementizers, as summarized in
(160).

Maximum specifier potential for the interrogative C in three types of
languages

(160)	$C_{0\text{-spec}}$	$C_{1\text{-spec}}$	$C_{m\text{-spec}}$
Japanese/Korean	$\checkmark$		
German		$\checkmark$	
English/Bulgarian			$\checkmark$

For Japanese, I rely mostly on data and insights from Miyagawa 1998.
For Korean (which I will not focus on), I rely on Beck and Kim 1996.

What do we expect from a language that must introduce *wh*-questions
with $C_{0\text{-spec}}$? Obviously, such a language will show *wh*-in-situ questions.
As is well known, Japanese and Korean are languages of this sort.

Wh-*in-situ (Japanese)*
(161) John-ga   nani-o   katta   no?
      John-NOM what-ACC bought Q
      'What did John buy?'

Wh-*in-situ (Korean)*
(162) Suna-ka   muŏs-ŭl   sass-ni?
      Suna-NOM what-ACC bought-Q
      'What did Suna buy?'

Except for differences in specifier potential, the interrogative complementizer used for *wh*-questions should be fundamentally identical across
languages. Consequently, we expect that Japanese and Korean $C_{0\text{-spec}}$,
like $C_{1\text{-spec}}$ and $C_{m\text{-spec}}$, bears an uninterpretable *wh*-feature. If this feature
is not deleted in the course of the derivation, the derivation should crash.
Since $C_{0\text{-spec}}$ does not allow *wh*-phrase movement to form a specifier, only
wh-feature movement (or its counterpart in the variant proposals discussed above) can delete its uninterpretable feature. Consequently, a
wh-question in such a language—be it a single question or a multiple
question—must contain at least one *wh*-phrase *not* separated from $C_{0\text{-spec}}$
by a scope bearer. If the question contains just one *wh*-phrase, and this
wh-phrase is separated from $C_{0\text{-spec}}$ by scope bearer, the question should
be unacceptable. As noted by Hoji (1985), this is indeed the case in
Japanese. A scope-bearing element in a single-*wh* question produces an

intervention effect whenever it comes between the *wh*-phrase and the interrogative complementizer. As in German, scrambling eliminates the violation, as the (b) examples show. ((163)–(166) are respectively from Tanaka 1999 (cited in Hagstrom 1998), Hoji 1985, Miyagawa 1998, and Hoji 1985; regarding (166), see also Hagstrom 1998.)

Intervention effect with wh *and negation/only (Japanese)*[100]

(163) a. *Hanako-sika nani-o   yoma-nai no?
           Hanako-only what-ACC read-NEG Q
           'What did only Hanako read?'
       b. Nani-o Hanako-sika yoma-nai no?

Intervention effect with wh *and* every *(Japanese)*[101]

(164) a. ?*Dono hito-mo nani-o   yonda no? [less deviant for some
            every person what-ACC read Q   speakers, allegedly
            'What did every person read?'   not necessarily with
                                                 wide-scope *every*]
       b. Nani-o dono hito-mo yonda no?

Intervention effect with wh *and* almost every *(Japanese)*

(165) a. *Hotondo dono hito-mo nani-o   yonda no? [for all speakers]
            almost every person what-ACC read Q
            'What did almost every person read?'
       b. Nani-o hotondo dono hito-mo yonda no?

Intervention effect with wh *and* or *(Japanese)*

(166) a. ?*[John-ka Bill]-ga nani-o   nomimasita ka?
            John-or Bill-NOM what-ACC drank   Q
            'What did John or Bill drink?'
       b. Nani-o [John-ka Bill]-ga nomimasita ka?

In essence, examples like the (a) sentences in (163)–(166) present the Japanese speaker with a Hobson's choice. If no feature movement takes place, the uninterpretable *wh*-feature in $C_{0\text{-spec}}$ is not deleted and the derivation crashes. If feature movement does take place, the result is an intervention effect. Quite comparable data have been provided for Korean by Beck and Kim (1996), for example.

Intervention effect with wh *and negative polarity item (Korean)*

(167) a. *Amuto muŏs-ŭl sa-chi   anh-ass-ni?
            anyone what-ACC bought-CHI not-did-Q
            'What did no one buy?'
       b. Muŏs-ŭl amuto sa-chi anh-ass-ni?

Intervention effect with wh *and* only *(Korean)*

(168) a. *Minsu-man nuku-lŭl poass-ni?
        Minsu-only who-ACC saw-Q
        'Who did only Minsu see?'

    b. Nuku-lŭl Minsu-man poass-ni?

Intervention effect with wh *and* every *(Korean)*

(169) a. ??Nukuna-ka   ŏnŭ kyosu-lŭl   chonkyŏngha-ni?
        everyone-NOM which professor-ACC respect-Q
        'Which professor did everyone respect?'

    b. Ŏnŭ kyosu-lŭl nukuna-ka chonkyŏngha-ni?

If the question contains multiple *wh*-phrases, the nature of the intervention effect is determined by the position of the intervener. When an intervener c-commands all *wh*-expressions, the same deviance results as in single *wh*-questions that have the same problem. ((170) is from Miyagawa 1997, citing Tanaka 1999. (170) is to be compared with (172).)

Intervener (only *) c-commands multiple* wh-*phrases (Japanese)*

(170) ?*Taroo-wa [Hanako-sika dare-ni nani-o   yom-ana-i   to] Tomoko-ni itta no?
        Taroo-TOP Hanako-only who-to what-ACC read-NEG-PRES C   Tomoko-to said Q
        'To whom did Taroo tell Tomoko that only Hanako read what?'

The cause of the deviance is the same as in the single-*wh* questions just examined. Either the complementizer is left with an undeleted *wh*-feature, or an intervention effect is produced.

When the intervener c-commands one but not all the *wh*-expressions in Japanese, the result is not deviant (Watanabe 1992; Tanaka 1999). (This is often known as the "additional *wh*-effect," following Saito 1994.) This is because *wh*-feature movement (or its counterpart in variant theories) can take place from the highest *wh*-phrase, eliminating the uninterpretable *wh*-feature on the complementizer. Nonetheless, the resulting sentences are limited to the single-pair reading, just as we have seen in English and German (Miyagawa 1997). The reason is the observation stated in (142), which characterizes the distribution of the single-pair reading in English and German.

Intervention effect in multiple questions with or *(Japanese)*

(171) a. ???John-ga   [MIT-ka Harvard]-ni nani-o   ageta no?
        John-NOM [MIT-or Harvard]-DAT what-ACC gave Q
        'What did John give MIT or Harvard?'

    b. Dare-ga   [MIT-ka Harvard]-ni nani-o   ageta no? [single-pair only]
        who-NOM [MIT-or Harvard]-DAT what-ACC gave Q
        'What did who give MIT or Harvard?'

Intervention effect in multiple questions with only *(Japanese)*
(172)

a. ?*Taroo-wa [Hanako-sika <u>nani-o</u>   yom-ana-i   to] Tomoko-ni itta no?
   Taroo-TOP Hanako-only what-ACC read-NEG-PRES C Tomoko-to said Q
   'What did Taroo say to Tomoko that only Hanako read?'

b. Taroo-wa [Hanako-sika <u>nani-o</u>   yom-ana-i   to] <u>dare-ni</u> itta no? [single-pair only]
   Taroo-TOP Hanako-only what-ACC read-NEG-PRES C who-to said Q
   'To whom did Taroo say that only Hanako read what?'

As in German, scrambling eliminates the intervention effect. ((173) is from Hagstrom 1998.)

Scrambling (Japanese)

(173) a. ?*[John-ka Bill]-ga dare-ni   nani-o   ageta no?
            John-or Bill-NOM who-DAT what-ACC gave Q
            'What did John or Bill give to who?'

   b. ?Dare-ni [John-ka Bill]-ga ____ nani-o ageta no?   [single-pair only]

   c. ??Nani-o [John-ka Bill]-ga dare-ni ____ ageta no?   [single-pair only]

   d. Dare-ni nani-o [John-ka Bill]-ga ____ ____ ageta no?   [pair-list reading OK][102]

In Korean similar facts seem to obtain—except that I have not investigated whether examples in which some but not all *wh*-phrases are c-commanded by the intervener have the single-pair reading. Beck and Kim (1996) mark such examples with an asterisk, which I reproduce here in square brackets. If the asterisk is real, even on a single-pair reading, the difference between Korean and Japanese will require further investigation.

Scrambling (Korean)

(174) a. *Amuto nuku-lŭl ŏti-esŏ   manna-chi anh-ass-ni?
            anyone who-ACC where-LOC meet-CHI   not-did-Q
            'Where did no one meet whom?'

   b. [*]Nuku-lŭl amuto ŏti-esŏ manna-chi anh-ass-ni?

   c. Nuku-lŭl ŏti-esŏ amuto manna-chi anh-ass-ni?

   d. Ŏti-esŏ nuku-lŭl amuto manna-chi anh-ass-ni?

As a final piece of reassurance, it is worth observing, with Miyagawa (1998), that Japanese displays the intervention effect in non-*wh* environments exactly where we expect to find it: in separation constructions. For example, when existential *dareka* 'some (adj.)' scrambles in a manner that strands its restriction, as in (175a–b), a scope-bearing phrase like 'only Hanako' may not intervene between *dareka* and its restrictor.

Intervention effect with Q-NP split (Japanese)
(175) a. Hanako-ga   gakusei-o   dareka yonda (koto)
        Hanako-NOM student-ACC some   invited (fact)
        '(the fact that) Hanako invited some student'
     b. $dareka_i$ Hanako-ga gakusei-o t_i yonda (koto)
     c. Hanako-sika gakusei-o   dareka yoba-nakat-ta (koto)
        Hanako-only student-ACC some   invite-NEG-PAST (fact)
        '(the fact that) only Hanako invited some student'
     d. *$dareka_i$ Hanako-sika gakusei-o t_i yoba-nakat-ta (koto)

Similar facts obtain when a numeral is scrambled away from its restriction.

Intervention effect with Num-NP split (Japanese)
(176) b. ?$San-satu_i$ Taroo-ga   gengogaku-no hon-o t_i yonda.
        3-CL   Taroo-NOM linguistics-GEN book-ACC   read
     d. *$San-satu_i$ Taroo-sika gengogaku-no hon-o t_i yoma-nakat-ta.
        3-CL   Taroo-only linguistics-GEN book-ACC   read-NEG-PAST

Japanese and Korean thus appear to meet our expectations for a language whose interrogative complementizer is identical to that of English and German, except that it does not take a specifier.[103] Since the notion of specifier potential played a crucial role in our original discussion of apparent AC violations, the results in this section help support conclusions we have already reached. The notion of specifier potential has been shown to play a key role in explaining variation in the syntax of *wh*-questions. In particular, the scale of specifier potential has been shown to correlate inversely with the number of environments in which *wh*-questions show intervention effects, as illustrated in (177).

Environments in which intervention effects are found in wh-*questions*

(177)	Single-*wh* questions	Multiple-*wh* questions	Multiple-*wh* questions with apparent AC violations
$C_{0\text{-spec}}$	√	√	√
$C_{1\text{-spec}}$		√	√
$C_{m\text{-spec}}$			√

This makes sense, since the fewer opportunities a language has for phrasal *wh*-movement, the greater the number of environments in which the restriction of a *wh*-phrase must remain inside TP, yielding intervention effects.[104]

5.6   Some Unanswered Questions about the Typology

Some important questions remain, to which the answers are not completely clear. One question concerns the repertoire of complementizers in a given language. I have described the list of available complementizers as fixed in the lexicon of each language. This is important to the action of the Complementizer Choice Rule in (141). If Japanese, for example, had the option of using $C_{m\text{-spec}}$ in a multiple question, the Complementizer Choice Rule should require its use in Japanese just as it does in English, where the forced use of $C_{m\text{-spec}}$ forms a key component of the explanation for the Superiority effect. As it happens, on one interpretation of Takahashi 1993, we may suspect that we are faced with exactly this problem.[105]

Though Japanese is famously a "*wh*-in-situ language," it allows *wh*-phrases to be fronted by a process that in certain cases has the properties of English or Bulgarian *wh*-movement, according to Takahashi. These properties show up when the *wh*-phrase is moved out of an embedded clause to the left periphery of an interrogative CP. For example, (178), in which *nani* 'what' has been fronted from a lower interrogative CP to the left periphery of a matrix interrogative CP, can only be understood as a matrix question. ((178) is Takahashi's (4b).)

Overt wh-*fronting in Japanese interrogative fixes scope*
(178) Nani-o   John-wa [CP Mary-ga _____ tabeta ka] siritagatteiru no?
     what-ACC John-TOP   Mary-NOM   ate   Q   want-to-know Q
     Only: 'What did John want to know whether Mary ate?'
     Not: 'Did John want to know what Mary ate?'

In all other cases *wh*-fronting has the properties expected from simple scrambling: "A-movement-like" properties when the fronting is more local (Webelhuth 1988; Mahajan 1990; Saito 1992), and reconstruction properties when the fronting does not target an interrogative CP. For example, (179) is identical to (178) except that the matrix clause is non-interrogative. In this case the fronted *wh*-phrase *nani* is understood via reconstruction as taking scope in the embedded clause. ((179) is based on Takahashi's (2b).)

Wh-*reconstruction with fronting in a noninterrogative clause*

(179) Nani-o   John-wa [$_{CP}$ Mary-ga ____ tabeta ka] siritagatteiru.
      what-ACC John-TOP   Mary-NOM   ate   Q   want-to-know
      'John wanted to know what Mary ate.'

The construction behaves as if the following statements were true of Japanese:[106]

• The left periphery of an interrogative CP may not be the target of long-distance scrambling of a *wh*-phrase.
• The left periphery of an interrogative CP may be the target of long-distance *wh*-movement.

Certain facts about this construction are murky. For example, Richards (1997) observes that multiple questions with two *wh*-phrases allow both *wh*-phrases to front, in which case his consultant noted a Bulgarian-style Superiority effect. Some speakers disagree with this judgment, even to the extent of finding (180b) marginally better than (180a).[107] ((180a–b) are from Richards (1997), citing a personal communication from Takako Aikawa.)

Bulgarian-style Superiority effect (Japanese)

(180) a. Dare$_i$-ni nani$_j$-o   Taroo-ga t$_i$ [Hanako-ga t$_j$ katta to] itta no?
          who-DAT what-ACC Taroo-NOM   Hanako-NOM bought C said Q
          'Who did Taroo tell that Hanako bought what?'
      b. *Nani$_j$-o dare$_i$-ni Taroo-ga t$_i$ [Hanako-ga t$_j$ katta to] itta no?

Takahashi notes the possibility of fronting only one of the two phrases and observes that a Superiority effect of the English sort arises here too. ((181) is from Takahashi 1993, 664.)

English-style Superiority effect (Japanese)

(181)

a. Dare-ni   John-ga [Bill-ga ____ [Mary-ga nani-o   tabeta to] itta to] omotteiru no?
    whom-DAT John-NOM Bill-NOM   Mary-NOM what-ACC ate   C said that thinks   Q
    'To whom does John think that Bill said that Mary ate what?'
b. *Nani-o John-ga [Bill-ga dare-ni [Mary-ga ____ tabeta to] itta to] omotteiru no?

Some controversy surrounds these observations as well. For one thing, the sharp cases of the "English-style" Superiority effect seem to involve situations like (181), in which one *wh*-phrase comes from a higher clause than the other. Other cases show weaker and more variable effects. If so, we might not be dealing with a Superiority effect at all in (181), but with a simpler contrast between longer- and shorter-distance scrambling—much as I suggested for German examples like (147a–b). Supporting this is the fact that multiple questions with left-peripheral *wh*-phrases do show an intervention effect when a scope-bearing element c-commands an unmoved *wh*-phrase in the question: a German pattern. If this is the case, then the analysis of Japanese must be more complex than represented so far. We must actually allow Japanese questions to be introduced by $C_{0\text{-spec}}$, $C_{1\text{-spec}}$, or $C_{m\text{-spec}}$: the first for in-situ questions, the second for questions like those in (181), and the third for "Bulgarian-style" questions like those in (180)—the Complementizer Choice Rule being somehow inactive in Japanese. Alternatively, we might continue to view the interrogative complementizer in Japanese as an instance of $C_{0\text{-spec}}$ and ask whether the attractor in putative overt *wh*-movement isn't a different entity entirely—perhaps an optional focus head above or below $C_{0\text{-spec}}$, which optionally takes multiple specifiers. For lack of clear and decisive evidence, I must leave the matter open.

A similar issue arises in French. Although French overall appears to display the English patterns of movement and pronunciation, it is well known that in matrix clauses French allows *wh* to remain in situ rather more freely than does English, without necessarily producing an "echo question" reading.

Matrix wh-*in-situ (French)*

(182) Ils   ont   rencontré qui?   [nonecho reading possible]
      they have met   who
      'Who did they meet?'

Chang (1997) and Bošković (to appear) have observed that *wh*-in-situ in this type of question shows the intervention effect. The examples in (183), from Chang 1997, are acceptable only as echo questions, as indicated by the annotation #.

Intervention effects (French)

(183) a. #Tous les étudiants ont rencontré qui?
            all   the students have met   who
      b. #Chaque étudiant a   rencontré qui?
            each   student has met   who
      c. #Il n'a pas rencontré qui?
            he has-NEG met   who

d. #Il admire   toujours qui?
   he admires always   who

f. #Personne n'   admire   qui?
   no-one   NEG admires who

If the intervention effect here is a sign that these matrix questions are introduced by $C_{0\text{-spec}}$, we once again need to ask whether the Complementizer Choice Rule is somehow inactive in French as well (with the English-style pronunciation pattern when $C_{m\text{-spec}}$ is chosen)—or whether $C_{0\text{-spec}}$ is perhaps the only option for the interrogative complementizer, with some other attractor, optionally absent from matrix questions, responsible for what we have hitherto thought of as *wh*-movement.[108]

Alternatively, $C_{0\text{-spec}}$ may be a special option related to the semantics of questions like (182). Boeckx (1999a,b) has argued that such questions are interpreted in a manner reminiscent of cleft sentences (e.g., *Who is it that you met?*)—with a strong presuppositional reading. *Personne* 'no one', for example, is not a felicitous answer to (182). If this is the case, we may suppose that French is in general like English in its use of interrogative complementizers, except for the special possibility of using $C_{0\text{-spec}}$ as a complementizer in strongly presuppositional single questions. This fact in turn might be compared with the fact that English (and French) allow $C_{1\text{-spec}}$ as the complementizer for D-linked multiple questions, as discussed earlier. Perhaps questions that are strongly context dependent quite generally allow complementizers with smaller than expected specifier potentials. I leave this line of thinking for further research.

Also left for further research is the possible existence of *pronunciation* patterns for multiple phrasal *wh*-movement besides those of English and those of Bulgarian. For example, I noted that the use of $C_{0\text{-spec}}$ to introduce a *wh*-question yields a question whose *wh*-phrases are pronounced in situ because they are in situ. The test of this hypothesis was the intervention effect. But there are other possible ways to derive a "*wh*-in-situ" language. One might imagine a language whose interrogatives could be introduced by $C_{1\text{-spec}}$ or $C_{m\text{-spec}}$—just like English—but in which *all wh*-phrases are pronounced in their pre-*wh*-moved position. (This is essentially the traditional proposal concerning *wh*-in-situ languages.) The sign of a "superficial" *wh*-in-situ language of this sort would be the absence of the intervention effect in simple *wh*-questions. As described by Aoun and Li (1993b), Chinese is such a language.[109]

Though open questions like these remain, I believe they do not challenge the arguments I have presented. These include the arguments for the existence of overt and covert phrasal movement as well as the relation I have called feature movement—though other views of this relation were also considered. The evidence for this position came from several sources, including ACD, intervention effects, and the typology of *wh*-constructions discussed in the previous paragraphs.[110] If successful, this study has filled in an important piece of the puzzle posed by *wh*-constructions—a puzzle whose solution illuminates the variety and nature of movement and its kin.

Notes

1. In later work Chomsky (1998) suggests a view of "feature movement phenomena" according to which movement per se is not part of the relation. I touch on this proposal in section 4.7.

2. Though not always. See Pesetsky 1997, 1998 for discussion of cases in which pronunciation targets more than one position in a movement construction.

3. I use *phrasal movement* as a cover term for movement of any syntactic unit that is word-sized or larger. Thus, what is traditionally called *head movement* is an instance of phrasal movement in my sense.

4. Larson and May's examples involve the matrix verb *want*. The phenomenon is clearer with negative verbs like *refuse* that make the scope of the quantified phrase entirely obvious.

5. In light of Müller 1996 and Müller and Sternefeld 1993, we must suppose that the c-command property is apparent because VP-fronting and *wh*-movement are in some fashion the same process. Where two movement processes are sufficiently different, the interaction with c-command is not observed (e.g., when scrambling and *wh*-movement yield a configuration in which a trace is not c-commanded by its antecedent).

6. The order of moved *wh*-phrases given here (*who what whom*) anticipates later discussion, but is irrelevant at this point.

7. A third approach, represented by Kayne 1998, reanalyzes apparent covert phrasal movement as overt movement masked by compensating overt movement of other constituents. On this view, for example, the derivation of *What did John give to whom?* might involve overt leftward movement of *what* to a position below *who* followed by leftward movement of the remnant IP containing traces of *what* and *to whom*. I will not investigate this alternative here. There is probably no straightforward translation of the proposals made in this book into this approach.

8. This proposal assumes that it is a property of the attracted element that causes movement to be phrasal rather than purely featural. Chomsky (1998) suggests an alternative: that it is a property of the attractor that causes movement to be phrasal (a property anachronistically called the *Extended Projection Principle (EPP) feature*; Chomsky 1981). In the end my proposal will more closely resemble

the one in Chomsky 1998, but this detail is not important at the present stage of the argument.

9. Chomsky's proposal leaves us with one style of phrasal movement, but does not explain why this style of movement involves the "overt" pronunciation pattern, as opposed to some other. Nunes (1995), Wilder (1999), and others have offered proposals, based on Kayne 1994, that fill this gap. Of course, if Chomsky's proposal is incorrect (as I argue here), then Nunes's and Wilder's proposals must be modified in some way. Both Nunes and Wilder explore interesting consequences of their hypotheses beyond the simple prediction of overt movement patterns, so it would be desirable to explore alternatives that retain these interesting results.

10. Brody (1995) independently develops a notion of "expletive-associate" chain whose properties are close to those one would need to attribute to the operation of feature movement in Chomsky's (1998) proposal. Unlike Chomsky, Brody (pp. 114–127) suggests a treatment of ACD compatible with his proposal that responds to some (but not all) of the evidence taken to support a treatment in terms of covert phrasal movement. In particular, he offers a proposal that responds to the scope evidence, but not to Fox's (1995) interpretation of the binding evidence in (7) (not available at the time Brody's work was written)—nor, obviously, to the new evidence presented here. He also expresses skepticism (p. 120) about the validity of the core fact—though a claimed counterexample (Brody's (50)) actually follows from Fox's proposal.

11. I owe these thoughts to a suggestion from Norvin Richards. See also discussion in Brody 1997.

12. The proposal bears interesting similarities to proposals within the Generalized/ Head-Driven Phrase Structure Grammar tradition (Gazdar 1981; Gazdar et al. 1985; Pollard and Sag 1994), which treat a wide variety of syntactic relations as the result of extremely local feature movement.

13. Kai von Fintel (personal communication) suggests that the effect may be weaker in *there* constructions that do not involve the verb *be* (judgment indications mine, but tentative).

(i) [??]There arose every problem that there could.

(ii) [??]On Tuesday, there didn't occur any of the disruptions that there did on Monday.

If this observation is correct, it may be related to the obligatory focus interpretation of the associate in a *there* construction without *be*. Conceivably the associate is actually extraposed from VP overtly, in the manner of heavy NP shift.

14. It is also worth noting that the copula does not block ACD. For example, the U.S. Army's recruiting slogan *Be all that you can be!* could have been offered in a form with ACD: *Be all that you can!*

15. Covert head movement might also fit the bill, except that overt cases of head movement generally obey strict locality conditions, whereas the movement discovered here (as discussed below) obeys very weak locality conditions. See Hagstrom 1998 for discussion and some competing considerations.

16. Because most *wh*-expressions may be understood as D-linked, it is hard to tell which among the *wh*-phrases in a multiple question must be D-linked for the Superiority effect to disappear. My own impression of speakers' judgments is that either the higher *wh*-phrase or the *wh*-phrase that moves overtly must be D-linked, but opinions differ. (For example, Comorovski (1996) claims that it is crucial for both the overtly moved phrase and the in-situ phrase to be D-linked.) I will try to sidestep this issue by referring sloppily to "D-linked questions" or "questions with D-linking," even though technically it is *wh*-phrases that are D-linked. Any attempt to explain the semantic sources of the syntactic properties of D-linking will require more conclusive investigation of this issue.

17. To my knowledge the effect seen in (33) was first noted by Kayne (1983), who offered an account in terms of his Connectedness principle—a proposed revision of the Empty Category Principle. Connectedness covers cases in which the highest *wh*-in-situ is not lexically governed (i.e., is a subject). However, the ameliorating effect of a "third" *wh*-phrase is not limited to those cases of the Superiority effect in which the highest *wh*-in-situ is a subject.

(i)   ??What did you persuade whom to give ____ to Mary?

(ii) What did you persuade who to give to whom?

By contrast, the variant of Connectedness that I proposed (Pesetsky 1982) did cover these cases, though I didn't say this explicitly. My observations about questions with three or more *wh*-phrases have been noted independently by Fiengo (1998).

18. I have encountered a few speakers who find (33b) less than perfect. All speakers acknowledge a contrast.

19. The double-asterisked examples in (35), (40), and (41) improve when the *wh*-in-situ is D-linked. I return to this fact later.

20. Some speakers of some Slavic languages report stronger effects of (37) than do others. There may be individual variation on this point—or crosslinguistic variation. Empirical work more fine-grained than I have undertaken is necessary.

21. Though it is tempting to imagine that clauses introduced with $C_{1\text{-spec}}$ uniformly receive a single-question interpretation and that clauses introduced with $C_{m\text{-spec}}$ uniformly receive a multiple-question interpretation, the facts will turn out to be somewhat more complex. In particular, certain multiple questions (in English and in other languages) appear to be introduced with $C_{1\text{-spec}}$.

22. Of course, one might continue to maintain that only a gradient (37) influences the judgment, by positing a nonlinear relation between number of violations and actual judgments. (An anonymous reviewer reports that comparable judgments in Serbo-Croatian are detectably gradient, without the major acceptability break reported here for Bulgarian.) In section 4.3, I argue that English multiple *wh*-questions with three or more *wh*-phrases are also instances of the phenomenon in (35). This argument will help settle the matter in favor of (36) and a nongradient (37).

23. This section mostly summarizes results reported by Richards (1997), whose work—along with Beck 1996—provided the inspiration for the research reported here.

24. As discussed later, the contrasts in (43) and (44) weaken in questions with D-linking. I have also encountered a few speakers who simply do not agree with the contrasts in (43) and (44), either finding all orders acceptable or reporting a hunch that particular intonation contours render the (b) examples acceptable, independent of D-linking. I have not been able to understand what factors distinguish the grammars of these speakers from the grammars of those who detect the judgments discussed here, nor have I been able to get to the bottom of the reports of an intonational difference.

Billings and Rudin (1994) identify several factors that license exceptions to the Superiority effect among their Bulgarian consultants. These include animacy and avoidance of phonetic identity. My informants and Richards's have not assented to the judgments reported by Billings and Rudin. Nonetheless, it is not impossible to imagine ways in which their data could be understood within the framework of hypotheses reported here, if considerations of animacy and phonetic identity are allowed to override the effects of Shortest Move. (I am grateful to Barbara Citko for bringing Billings and Rudin 1994 to my attention.)

25. Müller (1998), developing an optimality-theoretic approach to these phenomena, encodes this property directly as a constraint requiring "parallel movement"—movement that minimizes reversals of c-command. As far as I can tell, the approaches are empirically indistinguishable in this case.

26. It is worth noting that we might extend Chomsky's requirement to cover all instances of movement, both overt and covert, if the Y-model is abandoned, as suggested above.

27. As discussed in detail by Richards (1997), Bulgarian island effects are somewhat more complex than represented here. I have presented the Subjacency argument simply as a further demonstration of the PMC. The point most relevant here is the effect of the PMC on AC, as described above. Here again I have found some variability among speakers.

It should also be noted, as Günther Grewendorf (personal communication) has reminded me, that the condition that bars extraction from islands of adjuncts (or perhaps non-NPs) is not subject to the PMC. This may provide an argument that this condition has a nonsyntactic basis.

28. Bošković (1998, 1999) offers an alternative account of the ordering of Bulgarian triple *wh*-questions that does not extend to the Subjacency data just considered, but is compatible with the rest of this book. Like Richards, he assumes that multiple movement to the same head involves "tucking in." Like Richards and many others, he assumes that Superiority effects arise from a closeness condition on the operation Attract, an operation in which the featural needs of an attracting head are satisfied by copying some expression that can satisfy those needs.

Unlike Richards, however, Bošković suggests that when multiple *wh*-movement to the same C-system is observed, only the *first* instance of movement results from attraction of a *wh*-feature by an interrogative C. (An antecedent for this idea can be found in Cheng's (1991) theory that the first instance of *wh*-movement is special because it alone "types" the sentence as interrogative.) All other instances of movement to the specifier of that C are the result of featural needs intrinsic to the *wh*-phrases themselves (focus, perhaps)—not needs intrinsic to C. Thus, in a question that involves three *wh*-phrases, the first instance of *wh*-movement to C is a case of Attract, but the other two instances are cases of Move. When two *wh*-phrases have a need to move to [Spec, CP] in a clause in which a third *wh* (wh_1) has already been attracted to C, no principle regulates which of the two remaining *wh*-phrases moves first. That is why both $wh_1\ wh_2\ wh_3$ and $wh_1\ wh_3\ wh_2$ orders are possible. As far as I can tell, most of the results reported here are compatible with this hypothesis. Note, however, that *wh*-movement and focus movement must both target [Spec, CP] in Bulgarian. If the focus position were lower than C, the closest *wh*-phrase to C would be the highest *wh*-phrase in [Spec, Focus], and we would not expect to find the Superiority effect. This raises questions about focused non-*wh*-phrases, which are not freely interspersed among the fronted *wh*-phrases of a multiple question, as this approach would seem to predict.

29. This generalization clearly undermines a traditional argument for segregating covert movement into a component distinct from overt movement: their differing levels of obedience to subjacency. (The argument has also been made for cases of single-*wh* questions in languages like Chinese and Japanese, which also do not seem to show island effects. For a reanalysis of these cases, see Hagstrom 1998.) Despite this, Richards develops his PMC in the context of the Y-model and presents other arguments in support of that model. I will not evaluate these arguments here.

30. I will not derive this difference between English and Bulgarian from deeper properties of the grammars of these two languages.

In presenting this material, I have occasionally encountered the view that the absence of such a connection is a drawback of the proposal. As a spur to further research, such an objection can be useful. It is always possible that we will discover a crosslinguistic correlation between following (56) versus (57) and some other property of grammar. Furthermore, we will never discover such a correlation unless we look for it.

Nonetheless, as an a priori view, the objection is misplaced. Languages do differ, as a consequence of the role of linguistic experience in language acquisition. This fact means that certain differences among languages are virtually guaranteed to be irreducible. It is certainly possible (though not inevitable) that this is true of the language-particular choice between (56) and (57). The fact that the Germanic language Yiddish and the Romance language Romanian both show the Slavic pattern of (57) might support this view, by hinting that obedience to (57) does not depend too closely on other properties of syntax that distinguish the Slavic family of languages from its neighbors.

31. There is some controversy about whether string-vacuous *wh*-movement is possible (George 1980; Gazdar 1981; Chung and McCloskey 1983; Chomsky 1986a). I assume that it is. The opposite assumption would require nonlethal but substantial reformulations of my proposals.

32. Kai von Fintel (personal communication) suggests that this phenomenon may be related to an observation of Irene Heim's (personal communication to von

Fintel). I can offer a visitor a cup of coffee by asking "Would you like a cup of coffee?" Suppose the visitor finishes that cup and I want to offer him another. In this context I cannot simply repeat "Would you like a cup of coffee?", even though a standard semantics for indefinites allows this. I need to explicitly signal the fact that the question is a repetition by asking "Would you like *another* cup of coffee?" Repeated VPs (whether elided or not) may require explicit markers like *too* or *all* as part of the same phenomenon. The real puzzle becomes the absence of this requirement in relative clauses modifying quantifiers, as in familiar examples of ACD like (67a), where the addition of *also* actually makes the relative clause relatively unacceptable.

33. Taking up a suggestion made by Baltin (1987), Lasnik (1993) suggests that overt extraposition also resolves ACD in certain types of constructions. To simplify the discussion, I put this possibility aside.

34. As an anonymous reviewer suggests, on this view the impossibility of ACD in the associate of a *there* sentence, illustrated in (25), might be a consequence of assigning a kind of Case to the associate that does not require raising out of the VP—for example, what is sometimes called *inherent* Case.

35. If there is any phrasal movement for Case, we expect at least the availability of a reading in which Case-motivated movement of the outer bracketed DP permits ACD resolution in which the entire direct object is a variable (e.g., for (71b), the interpretation 'Melander requested copies of most of the tapes Larsson requested'). This is generally unavailable—which would be a good argument for the stronger position (that there is no phrasal movement for Case) were it not that QR also might be expected to allow this reading. If the outer bracketed DP undergoes QR (followed by secondary QR of the inner bracketed phrase), it creates a VP of the sort that could yield the unattested interpretation.

Though Kennedy (1997) discusses this issue at length—treating the possibility of double QR as a problem—Sauerland (1998b) notes that under certain circumstances this type of reading *is* available (perhaps marginally), especially when the inner and outer DPs contain identical material. *Bill visited a city near the city Mary did* thus seems to have two readings: 'Bill visited a city near the city that Mary visited a city near' and 'Bill visited a city near the city that Mary visited'. Space does not permit me to sketch Sauerland's proposal, but its logical structure is quite compatible with the proposals I make here.

36. This conclusion dovetails with an anonymous reviewer's observation that even predicates—expressions that seem not to need Case—may contain ACD (e.g., *I consider Bill everything that John doesn't*).

37. Perhaps the best argument I know in favor of this proposition is Wurmbrand's (1998) discussion of "restructuring" phenomena in German. She argues persuasively that infinitival complements to restructuring predicates are significantly smaller than CP or TP, and may be bare VPs. She then shows that although a bare VP complement to a restructuring predicate may contain a verb and its object, the licensing of object Case does not take place within this domain; instead, it depends on the Case properties of the restructuring predicate. The link

between the "smallness" of the embedded VP and the absence of objective Case licensing in that domain provides a good argument that objective Case licensing depends on VP-external structure.

38. A reviewer notes that if Case movement is feature movement, we face the task of explaining a set of differences between the feature movement posited for objective Case checking and the feature movement posited between T and the associate NP in the existential *there* construction. Several papers in Lasnik 1999 offer evidence from the binding theory, scope, and other phenomena that objective Case-marked NPs in English are interpreted outside the VP in which they originate. The same is not true of the nominative Case-marked NPs in the *there* construction. Their scope is confined to the VP (as in *There do not seem to be many linguists in the room*, where *many* unambiguously has scope lower than negation), as are their binding possibilities (*There seem to themselves to be some linguists in the room*). I will not try to resolve this difficulty here.

39. The only slender hope left for Case movement theories of ACD arises if we can argue that objective Case checking in general involves phrasal movement (overt or covert)—but that for some reason the pattern of *wh*-movement under study restricts objective Case checking to feature movement. I will not explore this possibility here.

40. As Kai von Fintel (personal communication) notes, the analyses of (74) and (75) actually coincide if one adopts the proposal by Larson, Den Dikken, and Ludlow (1997) (reminiscent of Generative Semantics) that posits clausal structure in the complement position of (75).

41. One weakness in this argument is the possibility that the Case position for the embedded subject lies outside the scope of *want* and licenses ACD, but the *de dicto* reading in (74a) results from either reconstruction or the scope neutrality of feature movement for Case reasons. (The latter suggestion is from Kai von Fintel (personal communication).) The reconstruction option in (74b) might be blocked by the ACD itself. The argument from (61a) does not have a comparable weakness.

42. In my (1987) theory of the Superiority effect, the very existence of D-linked counterexamples constituted an argument for the absence of covert movement of wh_1, since I assumed there that the Superiority effect arises from illicit configurations of covert movement, rather than from illicit choices for overt movement.

43. Chomsky's (1995) theory captures the inviolability of AC by building the condition into the definition of the operation Move.

44. An important terminological note: I will continue to use the informal term wh_1-*in-situ* to designate the highest of a group of *wh*-phrases when it has not undergone overt phrasal movement—regardless of whether *wh*-feature movement has taken place from it. *In situ* in this book means 'pronounced in situ'.

45. Covert phrasal *wh*-movement is not clause-bound. If it were clause-bound, examples like (i) would violate the multiple-specifier requirement, contrary to fact, and would have the same status as (ii).

(i) Who did Sue think bought what?

(ii) *What did Sue think who bought?

This result conflicts with a claim by Baltin (1987), who uses data from ACD as part of an argument that *wh*-in-situ does not undergo full phrasal movement of a sort that could resolve ACD. The example he cites is (iii) (his (14)).

(iii) Who thought that Fred read how many of the books that Bill did Δ?

According to Baltin, the ellipsis in (iii) may take the lower VP (... *read t*) as its antecedent, but not the higher VP (*... *thought that he read t*).

I believe that Baltin's factual claim is not correct (even though it is assented to by Kennedy (1997, 670), who suggests an account). True, there may be a preference for lower-clause interpretation of the ellipsis in examples like (iii), but the upper-clause interpretation does not seem to me to be excluded. Furthermore, no sensation of deviance arises when the context *forces* an upper-clause interpretation of the ellipsis—as in (iv) and (v), where the modal stranded before the ellipsis site matches a matrix modal and does not match material from the lower clause.

(iv) Which student will claim that you visited which woman that Mary (also) Δ will?

(v) Who might claim that he visited which city that Mary (also) Δ might?

It seems to me that the correlation between wide scope and the possibility of wide-scope ACD resolution holds up even in these cases.

46. Barss (to appear) claims that D-linked questions that (appear to) violate Superiority lack the pair-list reading otherwise available to multiple questions. If he is correct, a question like *Which book did which person buy?* can only seek for its answer a single person-book pair, such that the person bought the book—whereas the corresponding question that does not resemble a Superiority violation, *Which person bought which book?*, may seek a set of person-book pairs as its answer (*Mary bought this book, Bill bought that book*, etc.). If correct, Barss's claim would support my contention that apparent Superiority violations are possible only in the presence of a special type of interrogative complementizer, since we would be able to attribute a special semantics to this complementizer. Unfortunately, both types of multiple question seem to me to have a pair-list reading—particularly when contrasted with examples considered later (section 5.1) that strongly exclude the pair-list reading.

47. It would be useful to acquire evidence that could confirm or refute the claim that *wh*-in-situ in Bulgarian examples like (80a) (on the acceptable parse) does not undergo covert phrasal movement. To test this, we would have to develop evidence for something like VP-ellipsis in Bulgarian (which is not inconceivable: Stjepanović (1998) argues for the existence of VP-ellipsis in closely related Serbo-Croatian) and tests that can ensure that scrambling of complex NPs out of the VP has not taken place overtly. I have not undertaken this work.

48. This possibility turns the speakers who do *not* report any residual Superiority effect into the unexplained case, but perhaps these speakers are simply less sensitive to (37) than others are.

49. Roumyana Izvorski (personal communication) notes that the contrast is even clearer if the optional interrogative complementizer *li* is added.

(i)   **Na kogo koj li dade kakvo?

(ii) **Kakvo koj li dade na kogo?

(iii) *Na kogo kakvo li dade koj?

50. Curiously, if *koj* is placed to the left of the verb *dade* in (84), the result— though still unacceptable—improves once again.

(i)   a. ?*Na kogo kakvo koj dade?
      b. ?*Kakvo na kogo koj dade?

Perhaps (ia–b) are more acceptable than (83a–b) because they, like (84), have a parse in which *koj* has not undergone phrasal *wh*-movement, but remains (for pronunciation purposes, at least) in [Spec, TP].

(ii) a. ?*[$_{CP}$ Na kogo kakvo C$_{m-spec}$ [$_{TP}$ koj dade ___ ___]]?
      b. ?*[$_{CP}$ Kakvo na kogo C$_{m-spec}$ [$_{TP}$ koj dade ___ ___]]?

The difficulty with this proposal is that verb movement to C is normally obligatory in Bulgarian *wh*-questions, as in English.

(iii) a. *Na kogo   kakvo Ivan dade?
         to whom what Ivan gave
         'To whom did Ivan give what?'
      b. Na kogo kakvo dade Ivan?

All things being equal, this should render (ia–b) *worse* than (84)—not better. I leave this as a puzzle. I am grateful to Roumyana Izvorski for her judgments and to an anonymous reviewer for raising the issue.

51. The final *wh*-phrase in (85b) is included only to balance the corresponding phrase in (85a), but the judgment should remain constant even if it is eliminated: *What did who order [who that Mary (also) did Δ] to buy ___?*

52. As a reviewer points out, a proposal similar to this has been advanced by Barss (to appear). Barss suggests that the *wh*-feature on interrogative ("*wh*") phrases is optional, so that when a lower *wh*-phrase moves to [Spec, CP] over a higher *wh*-phrase left in situ, it is only because the higher phrase lacks the *wh*-feature. Barss does not discuss what ties this possibility to D-linking, but one might imagine extending his proposal as suggested in this (straw-man) paragraph.

53. In the present context Bošković's (1998, 1999) alternative to the PMC (see note 28) would do just as well.

54. It is in this limited sense that AC is "violable" even in my theory, though formally the "violations" actually accord with a general format for constraint satisfaction.

55. For me, *whom* is the obligatory form for object *wh*-in-situ, and *who* is the form for both objects and subjects when moved. As far as I can tell, the choice between *who* and *whom* makes no difference in this paradigm, except that for any given speaker the morphological rules followed by that speaker should be used in constructing examples.

56. It goes without saying that the PMC is conceptually surprising in its own right. Obviously, we would like to understand why the PMC holds. Nonetheless, for present purposes it is sufficient to view the PMC as a placeholder for a future explanation of the phenomenon. As long as the placeholder correctly identifies a real phenomenon, the significance of this discussion lies in the link it draws between otherwise distinct sets of facts in English and Bulgarian.

57. Of course, it could be argued that the notion of constraint ranking in OT is simply a different notion of what it means to be an "apparent" violation of a constraint. In any case, the issue is finding the correct account of the apparent violations. In lectures at the 1997 LSA Linguistic Institute at Cornell University, I presented an OT account of many of the phenomena subsequently analyzed as they are here. The proposal was a precursor to the present ones and included many of the components of this discussion, including the multiple-specifier requirement (with a D-linking exception) and AC. It also posited a MOVEMENT FAITHFULNESS constraint that favors derivations whose patterns of *wh*-movement and nonmovement match those of an "input" derivation. (In OT phonology, among the constraints governing pronunciation are some that favor "faithfulness" to an input form—in just this fashion. Only constraints ranked higher than a given faithfulness constraint can enforce a deviation from the input with respect to the property singled out by the faithfulness constraint.) MOVEMENT FAITHFULNESS strongly resembles the proposal made by Legendre, Smolensky, and Wilson (1998).

The ranking posited was this:

(i) MULTIPLE-SPECIFIER REQUIREMENT ≫ MOVEMENT FAITHFULNESS ≫ ATTRACT CLOSEST

MOVEMENT FAITHFULNESS occupies the same logical place in this OT proposal that the feature movement option occupies in the proposal presented here. It is what licenses apparent violations of ATTRACT CLOSEST, while not tolerating violations of the MULTIPLE-SPECIFIER REQUIREMENT. The system handled the data I have discussed as follows:

• Given an input derivation that violates the MULTIPLE-SPECIFIER REQUIREMENT (e.g., *What did who buy?*, with no covert movement of *who*), the MULTIPLE-SPECIFIER REQUIREMENT will reject it in favor of those alternative derivations in which at least two *wh*-phrases undergo movement, and ATTRACT CLOSEST will choose the one in which the highest *wh*-phrase moves first.
• Given a binary question in which the MULTIPLE-SPECIFIER REQUIREMENT is satisfied in the input (e.g., *Who bought what?*, with covert movement of *what*, or *What did who buy?*, with covert movement of *who*), MOVEMENT FAITHFULNESS will allow the input and all alternatives that share the same pattern of movement and nonmovement. ATTRACT CLOSEST will favor the one in which the highest *wh*-phrase moves first, even if that property was not met in the input.
• Given a nonbinary multiple question in which the MULTIPLE-SPECIFIER REQUIREMENT is satisfied, but wh_1 is not moved (e.g., *What did who give to whom?*, with covert movement only of *whom*), faithfulness will exclude derivations that satisfy ATTRACT CLOSEST, since they involve a movement pattern distinct from the

input, and ATTRACT CLOSEST, by the logic of OT, will be violated by the winning candidate.

To explain the facts just discussed in the text, it was necessary to stipulate that ATTRACT CLOSEST is nongradient. If presented only with candidates in which wh_1 remains in situ, so that the closest wh-phrase has not moved, ATTRACT CLOSEST "gave up" and enforced no preference among other movement possibilities. This property of ATTRACT CLOSEST could not be brought together with data handled by Richards's PMC, which I take to be a notable disadvantage of this OT account compared with its non-OT sibling defended here.

58. I am not, of course, providing a general argument against ranking and violability within the theory of movement—merely suggesting that one potential argument from Superiority violations does not support an OT view. Consequently, it might turn out that movement theory invokes a system in which constraints are ranked and violable that also countenances wh-feature movement as the first instance of movement in an apparent Superiority violation. Apparent Superiority violations would just not play a special role in arguing for the OT character of this system.

59. It is important to emphasize that the operation of wh-feature movement was not posited simply to maintain the view that AC is inviolable. It is also crucial to remember that the PMC considerations discussed in this section also converge on this conclusion.

60. One might add to the list semiarchaic *whence/thence* and *whither/thither*. I am grateful to Morris Halle for discussion of the morphological and phonological issues connected with the English wh-words. The parallelisms in (91) are, of course, not an original observation; they have frequently been noted in philological and other studies.

61. My phonological remarks should be understood as suggestions that the relation between putative underlying form and surface form could be the result of a natural process. I am aware that serious phonology imposes a higher standard of proof than my speculations meet.

62. The forms with *so-* are demonstratives distal with respect to speaker. The forms with *a-* are distal with respect to speaker and hearer.

63. This view might help us understand Chomsky's (1995) observation that certain instances of feature movement take other features along with them (as "free riders," in his terminology). The packaging of features in this way may reflect the distribution of morphemes in the language. For example, if Case and number are packaged together, as they typically are in Indo-European languages, we might expect that feature movement of Case also moves number.

64. The wh-morpheme discussed here seems to be quite distinct from the "Q-morpheme" on wh-phrases discussed at length by Hagstrom (1998). Hagstrom hypothesizes that the Q-morpheme is a quantifier over choice functions that moves to C to generate the observed interpretation for interrogative clauses. He argues that the Japanese morpheme *-ka*, usually identified as an interrogative

complementizer, is actually this morpheme after overt movement from a *wh*-phrase. The properties he identifies as properties of *-ka*, however, are quite orthogonal to the properties required of our *wh*-morpheme. For one thing, it appears to be present on only one *wh*-phrase in a multiple question, with some evidence that it appears only on the *lowest* of a group of *wh*-phrases when a multiple question receives a pair-list reading. It is strikingly hard to identify a semantic function for the *wh*-feature discussed here, at least within Hagstrom's framework. I leave this key issue for future study.

65. The mechanism by which the *wh*-feature percolates is unclear. In languages like Quechua and Basque, where clauses undergo pied-piping, the feature apparently percolates to larger constituents than is possible in English. Furthermore, the English conventions appear to be sui generis, which makes them hard to understand in terms of deeper principles. It appears that linear peripherality plays an important role. The basic rule for identifying an interrogative *wh*-phrase in English seems to be this:

(i) A *wh*-phrase has the form [(Adv) (P) *wh* . . .].

If the condition in (i) is met, the *wh*-feature can be embedded indefinitely far down in the structure.

(ii) a. Mary wondered [*wh*ose brother's cousin's shoes] we had found at the playground.
      b. *Mary wondered [the cousin of *wh*ose brother's shoes] we had found at the playground.

(iii) a. Mary wondered [in *wh*ose brother's cousin's shoes] we had been walking.
      b. *Mary wondered [in the cousin of *wh*ose brother's shoes] we had been walking.

(iv) a. Mary wondered [*how* many people's rights] the government had trampled on.
      b. Mary wondered [on *how* many people's rights] the government had trampled.
      c. Mary wondered [exactly *how* many people's rights] the government had trampled on.
      d. *Mary wondered [the rights of *how* many people] the government had trampled on.

(v)   a. Mary wondered [*wh*ich violinist's cadenzas] Kremer intended to play.
      b. *Mary wondered [the cadenzas by *wh*ich violinist] Kremer intended to play.

Perhaps the *wh*-feature adheres to a syntactic phrase by virtue of occupying the left periphery of the first phonological phrase of that constituent (on the assumption that leading prepositions and adverbs may have clitic status and do not need to belong to this phrase).

66. In OT terms we might think of the two principles as tied constraints (Pesetsky 1997, 1998).

67. For the details of the relevant conditions, Ochi follows Takahashi (1994). He argues, for example, that adjunction to individual members of multimember chains is forbidden by a general "uniformity" requirement on operations that affect chains. If subjects in [Spec, IP] have moved from a lower position, this requirement will predict the islandhood of subjects. Adjunct constituents that are semantically interpreted via coordination, including VP adjuncts and relative clauses, also bar adjunction. Thus, the islandhood of VP adjuncts and relative clauses is also predicted.

On one key point Ochi's hypotheses and mine are incompatible. Ochi follows Takahashi in arguing that the constraint on generalized pied-piping that requires extremely local landing sites is "mover-oriented" rather than "attractor-oriented." He suggests, in fact, that the relevant constraint is Shortest Move. If this were the case, we would expect the PMC to *never* license violations of island conditions, for the same reason it never licenses violations of the "tucking in" requirement (as discussed in the final paragraph of section 2.2). There is no "tax relief" from tucking in because Shortest Move is not a constraint governing the distance between an attractor and an attractee, but a constraint that chooses the exact position near a given attractor to which copying takes place. There is, as we have seen, "tax relief" from island conditions. Consequently, the two phenomena cannot both be traced back to Shortest Move.

68. If I were to substitute Agree for feature movement in my account of *wh*-configurations, the distribution of AC and Subjacency effects might be explained as follows:

1. Feature matching obeys AC, except insofar as the PMC allows exceptions.
2. Movement is subject to island conditions (Subjacency), except insofar as the PMC allows exceptions.
3. Movement of β to a specifier of α is possible only if a feature of α has been matched with a feature of β.

69. Needless to say, contexts in which the "good" examples are natural are often rather recherché. For example, (99a) requires a context in which the speaker knows that certain sensitive issues are to be avoided when speaking with certain diplomats.

70. This observation is similar to a point made by Beck (1996) for German.

71. There is also the (possibly distinct) functional reading, which I will ignore here. (It will ultimately be important to investigate these results in light of Chierchia's (1993) hypothesis that the pair-list reading is a species of functional reading.)

72. For very similar data and discussion, see Barss, to appear. Barss goes on to argue that the wide-scope answering pattern in examples like (108) does not include a pair-list reading for the two *wh*-phrases. Instead, the two *wh*-phrases are claimed to have an independent interpretation that, were it not for the universal quantifier *every*, would invite a single-pair response. This is in keeping with Barss's claim (disputed in note 46 above) that apparent Superiority violations of all sorts generally lack the pair-list reading—a claim at odds with the much sharper contrast between pair-list readings and their absence found with the intervention effect.

73. The illuminating contrast between *every* and *almost every* is adapted from Beck (1996), though she does not offer the explanation suggested here.

74. My statement contains the phrase *a clause interpreted as a question*, because if the question is embedded in further structure, wide-scope readings are available that do end up expressing requests for incomplete information or requests for no answer at all. Example (104) is a good case in point. On the other hand, the observation in (111) extends beyond the content of [Spec, CP]. For example, (i) cannot be a request for a partial list of people.

(i) #In part, who did Mary invite to the party?

However, (ii) may be a description of a partial answer.

(ii) John told me in part who Mary invited to the party.

75. One might imagine a question that requests an absence of an answer in a discourse in which it was conjoined with other questions. For example, one might imagine being able to use (i) to express the thought otherwise expressed by *Tell me which book Mary gave to John, but don't tell me which book anyone from Paris gave to John.*

(i) #Which book did Mary give to John, but which book did no one from Paris give to John?

The absence of this possibility is therefore of interest. Another unaskable question in the same vein is (ii).

(ii) Which problems did no one except Mary solve?

The question in (ii) can be a request for the names of the problems such that Mary solved them and no one else solved them. This is the narrow-scope reading for *no one except Mary*. The wide-scope reading for *no one* would amount to a request to keep quiet about who besides Mary solved problems, while providing the names of problems that Mary (possibly along with others) solved. A report of such a question, which would show *no one except Mary* taking higher-clause scope, might be something like (iii).

(iii) He was only interested in Mary's performance on the exam. He asked which problems no one except Mary solved.

Thinking about (iii) helps bring out the interest of the missing reading in (ii).

76. I embed the question under *tell me* because *each NP* does not easily allow wide scope over *wh* in a matrix question.

(i) Which book did each student buy ____? [? with a pair-list reading]

In this respect it behaves a bit like the quantifiers in (113). Perhaps "aggressively requesting" complete information within a question clause is not allowed, just as requests for incomplete information are not allowed. What the notion of "aggressively requesting" might be, such that it distinguishes *every* from *each* in the correct way, is unclear.

77. Counterevidence to this conjecture comes from Bulgarian, where the one consultant I have asked (Roumyana Izvorski) reports neither marked unacceptability nor loss of the pair-list reading when a D-linked *wh*-in-situ is separated from interrogative C by negation. Recall that Bulgarian allows *wh*-phrases to

appear in situ when they are D-linked. I argued in section 4.2 that these phrases are truly in situ, in the sense that their link to C involves feature movement, rather than phrasal movement. Izvorski does report that (i) is somewhat worse than (ii).

(i) [?]Koj ne dade kakvo na Stefan?
    who not gave what to Stefan
    'Who did not give what to Stefan?'

(ii) Koj dade kakvo na Stefan?

However, she also reports that (iii) is a bit worse than (iv), making it impossible to confidently attribute the constrast between (i) and (ii) to the intervention effect discussed in the text.

(iii) [?]Koj kakvo ne dade na Stefan?
     who what not gave to Stefan

(iv) Koj kakvo dade na Stefan?

It is conceivable that Bulgarian reveals a genuine flaw in my characterization either of the special effects of D-linking or of the intervention effect. It is also possible that other factors are masking the expected effect. For example, the degradation observed in (iii) might indicate that negation in Bulgarian has scopal properties (e.g., obligatory widest scope) that, on the one hand, interfere with multiple questions altogether and, on the other hand, bypass the intervention effect. I leave this as an open problem for the hypotheses advanced here.

78. If the Agree alternative to feature movement is adopted, then it is the mere fact that the restriction remains within TP (the "nuclear scope"), rather than the existence of separation, that produces the effect. All my generalizations remain intact.

79. Beck also observes an intervention effect with the German "partial movement" construction. The partial movement construction is a form of interrogative whose [Spec, CP] contains an invariant *was* 'what', and the *wh*-phrase that would otherwise occupy that [Spec, CP] is instead found in some lower [Spec, CP]. For example:

(i) Was glaubst du, mit wem Hans gesprochen hat?
    what believe you with whom Hans spoken   has
    'Who do you believe that Hans spoke to?'

The intervention effect shows itself in examples like these, from Beck 1996:

(ii) *Was glaubst du nicht, mit wem Hans gesprochen hat?
     what believe you not   with whom Hans spoken   has
     'Who do you not believe that Hans spoke to?'

(iii) [22]Was glaubt niemand, wen Karl gesehen hat?
      what believes nobody whom Karl seen   has
      'Who does nobody believe that Karl has seen?'

(iv) [22]Was glaubt fast   jeder,   wen Karl gesehen hat?
     what believes almost everyone whom Karl seen   has
     'Who does almost everyone believe Karl has seen?'

Cheng (1997, to appear) has argued that partial movement in German involves phrasal movement followed by feature movement of the *wh*-feature (a conclusion that may dovetail with Cole and Hermon's (1998) demonstration that the relationship between the *wh*-phrase and the invariant interrogative marker obeys island conditions in Malay). If we adapt this hypothesis to the overall account I have proposed, we might handle the effects seen in (ii)–(iv) in the same way as the effects discussed in the text.

80. The well-known constraint on separation of French *combien* 'how many' from its restriction discovered by Obenauer (1984) is presumably an instance of the intervention effect in a separation construction (see also Rizzi 1990).

(i) a. [Combien de véhicules] a-t-il conduit ____?
         how-many of cars   did he drive
         'How many cars did he drive?'
     b. Combien a-t-il conduit [____ de véhicules]?

(ii) a. [Combien de véhicules] n'a-t-il pas conduit ____?
         how-many of cars   did-he not drive
         'How many cars didn't he drive?'
     b. *Combien n'a-t-il pas conduit [____ de véhicules]?

As noted by Longobardi (1986), among others, similar effects can be detected in English, when attention is paid to the relative scope of the *many NP* portion of *how many* questions with respect to scope markers. This shows that the intervention effect is sensitive to reconstruction phenomena, not a surprise for a condition on LF.

81. I am extremely grateful to Jim McCloskey for collecting these data, which represent the judgments of a number of West Ulster English speakers gathered in San Francisco. He writes (personal communication):

The effect is weakest for simple negation as in [(130a)]. Everyone was very clear about [(130b,d,e)], but about [(130a)] there was more doubt and more debate (people began making up elaborate scenarios about shopping lists etc). [(130b,d,e)] are uninterpretable, but interpretations can be constructed for [(130a)]. The interpretation which is available is, in my opinion, one in which the *wh*-phrase is strongly D-linked.

The interpretation that is available for [(130c)] is, in my opinion anyway (though the people I was working with couldn't articulate this), one in which the subject quantifier has wider scope than the *wh*-phrase (i.e. for every relevant person, give me a complete listing of the things they got on Christmas morning). The other scope (*wh* > *every*) is incoherent with [(130c)].

As McCloskey (2000) notes, the phenomenon of *wh-all* separation is of more general interest, especially because the *all* may be stranded in what appear to be intermediate [Spec, CP]s. For more discussion, see McCloskey 2000.

82. As already noted, one also wants to know why the intervention effect exists. Considerations advanced by Reinhart (1997) suggest a possible line of attack, though some rethinking is necessary. Reinhart states that in Pesetsky 1987 I propose that all D-linked *wh*-in-situ are interpreted in situ, rather than by covert phrasal movement. She then shows that on the simplest assumptions about in-situ interpretation of *wh*-phrases, this suggestion fails. In particular, in a downward-

entailing environment, if we interpret the restriction on a *wh*-phrase as a conjunction at the lowest possible level, multiple questions should allow all manner of silly answers—for example, *Lucie will invite Donald Duck, and Bill will invite Mickey Mouse* in (i)–(ii).

(i) Who will be offended if we invite which philosopher?
    a. i. *Wrong interpretation*
        For which $\langle x, y \rangle$, if we invite *y* and *y* is a philosopher, then *x* will be offended?
      ii. *Answer*
        Lucie–Donald Duck; Bill–Mickey Mouse; ...   [i.e., Lucie will be offended if [DD is a philosopher and] we invite DD.]
    b. *Right interpretation*
      For which $\langle x, y \rangle$, *y* is a philosopher, and if we invite *y*, *x* will be offended?

(ii) Which linguist didn't invite which philosopher?
    a. i. *Wrong interpretation*
        For which $\langle x, y \rangle$, *x* is a linguist & [it is not the case that *y* is a philosopher and *x* invited *y*]?
      ii. *Answer*
        Lucie–Donald Duck; Bill–Mickey Mouse
    b. *Right interpretation*
      For which $\langle x, y \rangle$, *x* is a linguist & *y* is a philosopher & [it is not the case that *x* invited *y*]?

On the one hand, Reinhart is not correct about the details of my (1987) proposal. In that paper I argue that D-linked *wh may* (not "must") be interpreted in situ. Nonetheless, one wonders whether—in those cases where the only parse for a multiple question involves *wh*-feature movement—the deviance attributed to the intervention effect might actually be attributable to the "Donald Duck" problem. It is necessary to imagine that questions that fail to control their answers are actually felt as deviant—which of course is the sticking point here. Nonetheless, if this conjecture is correct, Reinhart's observation may have (semi-inadvertently) provided the key to understanding the intervention effect. That is, she may be correct in her argument that in-situ restrictions cause interpretive difficulties, but wrong in her assumption that this poses a problem for theories that allow for in-situ interpretation. It might instead offer a solution to a problem: why the intervention effect holds. Unfortunately, this proposal does not cover cases of the intervention effect involving interveners like *every*, which are not downward entailing for their nuclear scope. If these cases are of a piece with the others, Reinhart's suggestion is not apropos here. Honcoop (1998) offers an alternative that might be investigated in its place.

83. In principle, any sort of antecedent-contained anaphora could be used to discover whether a restriction on a quantifier or *wh*-phrase exits its VP by means of covert phrasal movement. For example, one might hope that antecedent-contained clausal anaphora as in (i) can be taken as a probe of the appropriate sort, where *that* seems to take a clause of the form *PRO invite t* as its antecedent.

(i) John wanted to invite exactly those people who didn't want him to do that.

If this type of anaphora could provide a test akin to ACD, we could use this test in languages like German that do not allow VP-ellipsis. Unfortunately, this type of anaphora differs from VP-ellipsis in allowing a variety of contextually salient antecedents, including entirely nonlinguistic ones. For example, *that* in (ii) can take a visually presented action as its antecedent.

(ii) I wish you wouldn't do that!

As discussed earlier, the inability of VP-ellipsis to take antecedents not present in the linguistic environment is crucial to the link between ACD and covert phrasal movement. In fact, such a link seems to be absent for clausal anaphora. An argument that ACD could only be resolved by movement came from Larson and May's (1990) facts discussed in (5). In (5) it was crucial that the elided VP in (iii) cannot take the higher VP headed by *refuse* as its antecedent without the *every* phrase taking wide scope.

(iii) John refused to visit [every city Mary did [$_{VP}$ Δ]]. [*cannot mean:* John refused to do the following thing: visit every city Mary refused to visit.]

Since the referent of clausal anaphora does not have to be present in the linguistic environment, it can be merely "evoked" by the linguistic environment. Consequently, we do not find the link between scope and antecedent-contained anaphora seen in (iii).

(iv) John refused to call every employee who wanted him to do that. [*can mean:* John refused to do the following thing: call every employee who wanted John to refuse to call him.]

84. The observation is due to Beck (1996), who does not, however, develop an account of the contrast with English.

85. Beck (1996, 3, fn. 2) offers a more nuanced description of the unacceptability judgment:

The "$\frac{??}{}$" means that the data are incomprehensible (uninterpretable) rather than simply ungrammatical. I would accordingly ask native speakers to try and interpret the sentences, not simply judge whether they "sound bad."

Some English speakers describe much the same effect. Though Beck does not mention the improved acceptability with a single-pair reading in her (1996) article, it was she who first mentioned the fact to me, in the context of German.

86. If the Agree variant is correct, they have in common with separation constructions the presence of the restriction on quantification inside the nuclear "scope" (the main body of the clause). See note 78.

87. For example, one might be tempted to argue that the presence of separation constructions in German that are not allowed in English indicates a greater overall "separability" of the components of *wh*-phrases. If feature movement or morpheme movement is favored over phrasal movement, this greater overall separability might yield (138). As far as I can tell, however, languages and dialects differ substantially in the availability of separation constructions in ways that do not correlate with (138). For example, the Slavic languages show a wide variety of

separation constructions yet allow multiple phrasal movement, as we have seen in Bulgarian.

88. I state (141) informally because its place in the overall scheme of things is underdetermined by the available facts. The Complementizer Choice Rule might be part of the theory of merger in a bottom-to-top derivation, in which case a more careful formulation might be as follows:

(i) Consider a TP τ that contains n instances of *wh* not moved to its scope position. An interrogative complementizer κ with specifier potential m may merge with τ only if the lexicon contains no interrogative complementizer κ' with specifier potential p, such that $m < p \leq n$.

This formulation has the odd result of ruling out extraction of a *wh*-phrase from a nonmultiple embedded question (but not from an embedded multiple question); that is, it attributes one, but not all, of the cases of the *Wh*-Island Constraint to the principle of complementizer merger. If this consequence is false, one should look for alternative hypotheses.

For example, the rule could also be understood as a filter on *wh*-movement, along the following lines:

(ii) An interrogative complementizer κ with specifier potential m may attract n instances of *wh* only if the lexicon contains no interrogative complementizer κ' with specifier potential p, such that $m < p \leq n$.

I leave the investigation of these possibilities and others for further research.

89. The Complementizer Choice Rule as stated in (141) is compatible with the treatment of D-linked questions offered in (79). According to (79), the central peculiarity of D-linked *wh* lies in the fact that feature movement from a D-linked *wh* can satisfy a requirement of $C_{m\text{-spec}}$ that is otherwise satisfiable only by phrasal movement. I also considered an alternative to (79) according to which the exceptional feature of questions with D-linking is different: they allow a multiple-question interpretation with $C_{1\text{-spec}}$. If the alternative is on the right track, we do not need (79), but D-linked questions are some kind of exception to (141). As noted earlier, more work is needed before we can understand (rather than merely describe) why *wh* with the semantics of D-linking has the syntactic peculiarities that it does. (I owe these points to discussion with Norvin Richards.)

90. The truth is more complicated. In addition to cases that I turn to in the next paragraph, certain types of *wh*-phrases do seem to yield a Superiority effect. For example, as Armin Mester (personal communication) notes, phrases of the type that I called "aggressively non-D-linked" in Pesetsky 1987 yield something like a Superiority effect. Judgments differ, but many speakers report a contrast between examples like (ia) and (ib)—a discovery independently reported by Wiltschko (1997). (The examples are Wiltschko's.)

(i) a.   Wer zum   Teufel hat wen   gesehen?
       who to-the devil   has whom seen
       'Who the devil saw whom?'
   b. ?*Wen zum Teufel hat wer gesehen?

Conceivably it is wrong to argue, as I have, that German lacks $C_{m\text{-spec}}$ entirely. Instead, it is possible that German reserves $C_{m\text{-spec}}$ in multiple questions for explicitly non-D-linked questions (with $C_{1\text{-spec}}$ as a default) as a mirror image of the fact that English reserves $C_{1\text{-spec}}$ in multiple questions for explicitly D-linked questions (with $C_{m\text{-spec}}$ as a default).

There are a few other ways to bring out a Superiority effect in German. Haider (2000) notes that it is unacceptable to overtly move a *wh*-phrase over another *wh*-phrase when the two are identical. The verb *beten* 'ask', unlike *versprechen* 'promise', takes an accusative object.

(ii) a. Wen   hat er denn *wem*   versprochen [davan ____ abzuhalten]?
         whom-ACC has he PRT   whom-DAT promised   from-it   to-keep-away
         'Who did he promise to keep whom away from it?'   [translation reverses the
         movement pattern]

     b. *Wen   hat er denn *wen*   gebeten [davan ____ abzuhalten]?
         whom-ACC has he PRT   whom-ACC asked   from-it   to-keep-away

I have no account for this fact.

91. Wiltschko (1997) offers another interesting problem for this conclusion. Consider a multiple question with two *wh*-phrases in which both phrases are taken to range over the same set containing two individuals. In German such a question yields a Superiority effect.

(i) Peter is walking his stubborn dog on the leash. The dog is dragging really
     hard in the direction of his favorite tree.

     a. Wer führt denn hier wen   an der Leine?
         who leads PRT   here whom on the leash
         'Who is leading whom here on the leash?'

     b. *Wen führt denn hier wer an der Leine?

(ii) I have heard that Peter and Mary had an affair. Can you tell me:

     a. Wer hat wen   verführt?
         who has whom seduced
         'Who seduced whom?'

     b. *Wen hat wer verführt?

(iii) I am sure that Peter and Mary must have talked to each other on the phone.

     a. Weißt du, wer wen   angerufen hat?
         know you who whom called   has
         'Do you know who called whom?'

     b. *Weißt du, wen wer angerufen hat?

One can imagine ways in which such questions might differ syntactically from other questions to yield these effects, but the solutions that come to my mind are mechanical. For example, in English the *wh*-phrase that moves overtly in other multiple questions has a special status as the "sorting key" for the answer (Kuno 1982). Thus, a person who asks *Which person bought which book?* normally expects an answer that exhausts some domain of people, but not necessarily any domain of books, whereas the person who asks *Which book did which person buy?* normally has the opposite expectation. No such difference can be imagined in

Wiltschko's cases, where the expected answer naturally exhausts the relevant set no matter what. Suppose the requirement of a *wh*-specifier needs to be satisfied as early as possible in the derivation, except when delaying the requirement makes an interpretive difference. Such a condition on the patterns of movement might account for Wiltschko's observation, since the (b) examples, if I am correct, show feature movement preceding phrasal movement.

92. Previous proposals link the absence of Superiority effects with subject *wh*-in-situ to the absence of *that*-trace effects in German (e.g., Haider 1986; see also Müller 1995). My proposal does not make this link.

93. I am grateful to Irene Heim (personal communication) for this observation. Furthermore, if a higher clause is added to (147) so that even (147a) involves *wh*-movement from an embedded clause, three of five speakers polled found that the difference disappeared. Two speakers still felt that (147b) remained less acceptable, but one volunteered the observation that *wh*-extraction from one finite clause (as in (147a)) is in general more acceptable for her than extraction from two finite clauses (as in (147b)).

(i) a. ??/*Wer denkst du, daß ____ glaubte, daß der Peter when   vorstellte?
           who think   you that   believed that the Peter whom introduced
     b.   *Wen   denkst du, daß wer glaubte, daß der Peter ihr   ____ vorstellte?
           whom think you that who believed that the Peter to-her   introduced

A particularly interesting case might be provided by Dutch, if the status of the Superiority effect for Dutch speakers can be resolved. Some Dutch speakers, at least, present judgments on the Superiority and intervention effects that are identical (or nearly so) to those reported for German, with three exceptions. First, Dutch lacks a scrambling process that places objects to the left of subjects (Johnson and Tomioka 1997). Second, interrogative *wh*-phrases move freely from embedded finite clauses. Third, Dutch fails to display the contrast in (147) (Sjef Barbiers, personal communication). For these speakers, one might argue that scrambling does not provide the explanation for the phenomena discussed here. Koster (1987, 204) and Aoun et al. (1987, ex. (61)) do note a contrast between Dutch equivalents of *Who saw what?* and *What (did) who see?* that looks like a Superiority effect. Although the judgment reported by Aoun et al. is assented to by van de Koot (1988), Koster expresses doubts about the strength of the effect (p. 236, fn. 12). Concerning (i), he writes, "I find it difficult to make up my mind. . . . The sentence does not seem entirely ungrammatical, which again casts doubt on the generality of the proposed explanations [in terms of a Superiority effect]." (Koster himself cites (ii) without an asterisk, though earlier he asterisks a comparable example.)

(i) Wat heeft wie gekocht?
    what has   who bought

As Günther Grewendorf (personal communication) points out, it is also worth noting that Bulgarian shows Superiority effects despite also allowing scrambling, as perhaps (according to Grewendorf) does Turkish. Japanese (discussed here in section 5.5) provides a similar case. Thus, there does not appear to be a correlation between the availability of scrambling and the apparent absence of Superiority effects.

94. Beck (1996) notes that *wh* may appear to the left of a subject if it is quantified—perhaps a (mysterious) instance of the otherwise forbidden scrambling of *wh*-phrases, as suggested by Sauerland (1996). If so, (i) is a counterexample to the generalization given in the text.

(i) Wer hat gesagt, daß wen   niemand mag?
    who has said   that whom-ACC nobody   likes
    'Who said that nobody likes whom?'

95. The translations of (150a–b) and (151a–b) are, of course, not fully acceptable English, since they show the Superiority effect—but there are no fully acceptable alternatives.

96. Kai von Fintel (personal communication) reports that extraction from the embedded clause *without* separation is degraded, to a level better than (152c) but worse than (152b). I do not know why this is the case. It is also worth noting that the *who of NP* construction does not display the same contrast as that seen in (152) and (153). This might be due to the possibility of taking the PP to modify the clause ('among the musicians, . . .') in clause-initial position.

97. I quote Fanselow's data here. Some speakers dislike extraction from the object of certain verbs, including *kritisieren* 'criticize'. Such speakers should judge comparable examples with a variety of main verbs.

98. Günther Grewendorf (personal communication) notes that many German speakers entirely lack Weak Crossover effects with *wh*-phrases, so a strong burden would fall on the claim that such effects are generally stronger with feature movement. Wiltschko (1997, 125) notes speaker variation in weak crossover judgments. I will not tackle this problem here.

99. Also relevant are examples like (i), which should be compared with the examples discussed in section 3.1.

(i) ?*I need to know [which girl that Mary did Δ] Sue ordered which boy to
        congratulate ____.   [i.e., I need to know the girl-boy pairs such that both
        Sue and Mary ordered the boy of the pair to congratulate the girl of the
        pair]

The example cannot be ruled out by any failure of ACD, per se, since the deletion site has undergone overt movement. The problem seems to be the fact that *which boy* fails to c-command a variable that it must bind within the deletion site, and feature movement seems to fail to allow this binding.

100. Beck and Kim (1996) provide similar examples from Korean.

(i) a. *Amuto nuku-lŭl po-chi anh-ass-ni?
        anyone who-ACC see-ing NEG-did-Q
    b. Nuku-lŭl amuto po-chi anh-ass-ni?

101. Miyagawa (1998) notes that the choice of quantifier makes a difference here. In particular, *minna* 'every' does not produce the intervention effect—one of many

differences between *minna* and other universal quantifiers discussed by Miyagawa. I will not attempt to account for this fact here.

102. The order of fronted *wh*-phrases matters. If the order is switched, as in (i), only a single-pair reading is possible.

(i) Nani-o dare-ni [John-ka Bill]-ga ____ ____ ageta no?   [single-pair only]

This is expected if one of the scrambled *wh*-phrases must reconstruct, but it is unclear why that would be the case. Perhaps if *nani-o* had to be parsed as an instance of "Ā-scrambling" like instances of long-distance scrambling (Webelhuth 1988; Mahajan 1990; Saito 1992), reconstruction would be forced, as suggested by Paul Hagstrom (personal communication). I leave the problem unresolved here.

103. Günther Grewendorf (personal communication) points out that *wh*-in-situ appears to generate an intervention effect in German separation constructions.

(i) Was hat der Professor den Studenten [____ alles] geraten?
    what has the professor the students   all   advised
    'What-all did the professor advise the students?'

(ii) *Was hat wer den Studenten [____ alles] geraten?
     what has who the students   all   advised

As he notes, this fact is a problem for my hypotheses concerning Japanese. If all Japanese *wh*-phrases associate with C via feature movement, then the higher of two *wh*-phrases in a multiple question might be expected to block the existence of the lower, just as *wer* in (ii) blocks the separation of *was* from *alles*. I leave this issue open; perhaps the set of interveners is not quite the same in Japanese as it is in German—as argued by Beck and Kim (1996) with respect to Korean and German.

Another open question noted by Grewendorf concerns subjacency. I observed in section 4.7 that the hypothesized *wh*-feature movement in English does not show island effects of the sort usually attributed to the Subjacency Condition and does not pay a "Subjacency tax" for later instances of phrasal *wh*-movement. If Japanese *wh*-in-situ always associate with interrogative C by *wh*-feature movement, one might expect them also to disobey Subjacency and not to pay a "Subjacency tax." This is true up to a point. *Wh*-phrases quite generally fail to show Complex NP Constraint effects, but they do show *Wh*-Island effects, as documented by Watanabe (1992). In addition, they do pay a "Subjacency tax" (governed by the PMC) for *wh*-island violations, as Watanabe also documents. *Wh*-feature movement of *dare-ni* in (iv) to the matrix complementizer *no* permits subsequent feature movement from *nani-o* to the matrix complementizer to avoid the *Wh*-Island effect seen in (iii).

(iii) ??John-wa [Mary-ga nani-o   katta ka dooka] siritagatte-iru no?
      John-TOP Mary-NOM what-ACC bought whether   know-want   Q
      'What does John want to know whether Mary bought?'

(iv) John-wa [Mary-ga nani-o   katta ka dooka] dare-ni   tazuneta no?
     John-TOP Mary-NOM what-ACC bought whether   who-DAT asked   Q
     'Who did John ask whether Mary bought what?'

It is not clear how we should understand the contradiction between the distribution of island effects in Japanese and the observations in the text concerning feature movement in English. It is possible that this contradiction reveals some fundamental problem with the hypotheses advanced here. It may also be the case that the contradiction simply reveals how the PMC individuates syntactic relations. In (iv) we observe (if my ideas about Japanese are correct) an instance of feature movement rescuing another instance of feature movement from Subjacency effects. In (95)–(97), by contrast, we were examining cases in which an instance of feature movement might have been expected to rescue an instance of phrasal movement. This might make a difference, but I will leave the question open for now.

104. Beck (1996) and Beck and Kim (1996) suggest a different crosslinguistic predictor for the intervention effect. They note that both Korean and German (the languages they discuss) allow scrambling to remove a *wh*-phrase from the scope of a potential intervener, whereas English does not. They suggest that if a language has a scrambling process that can eliminate an intervention effect, it must use it— and they speculate that the absence of scrambling correlates with the absence of the intervention effect. For them, the intervention effect is an island condition on traces of movement that have not been formed as early in the derivation as possible. It thus restricts "LF traces" in a language like German or Korean where scrambling can yield an overt-syntax trace in the same environment, but remains silent about comparable "LF traces" in a language like English, where no overt process can create the trace earlier in the derivation. (As Beck and Kim note, the logic here follows the Earliness Principle (Pesetsky 1989); also see Diesing 1992.) However, they do not note the intervention effect with which this discussion began: the English effect found in multiple questions that appear to violate AC. One can imagine variants of their approach that might accommodate the intervention effect in English, but none of these (I think) straightforwardly extends to the other properties of these constructions discussed earlier.

105. This issue was brought to my attention by Hisatsugu Kitahara. I am also grateful to him for discussing the issue with me at length.

106. Hasegawa (1994) shows that a similar paradigm holds for the interaction of scrambling and negation with the negative polarity suffix -*sika* 'only' and with -*mo* 'also'. One wonders if a language could have the properties identified by Hasegawa without the property identified by Takahashi, and vice versa.

107. Disagreement of this sort is not unknown among Bulgarian speakers either, as noted earlier. Shigeru Miyagawa (personal communication) suggests that the contrast emerges most clearly when one focuses on the pair-list interpretation for the two examples. In his judgment (180b) and (181b) have only single-pair readings.

108. A similar speculation has been advanced by Miyagawa (1998).

109. I owe this suggestion to Norvin Richards (personal communication). Aoun and Li relate the Japanese/Chinese difference to morphological differences in their *wh*-words. In a footnote they observe an important difficulty: Korean patterns

with Chinese morphologically (by allowing bare *wh*-words to serve noninterrogative functions), but patterns with Japanese in showing the intervention effect. My speculation about Chinese entails that Chinese *wh*-phrases, unlike their Japanese counterparts, undergo covert phrasal movement. This contradicts the conclusions of Aoun and Li (1993a) and other researchers, such as Tsai (1994).

110. It will be interesting to investigate similar typologies in other domains. There are some intriguing possibilities. Guerzoni (1999) investigates whether the licensing of negative polarity items (NPIs) in English and Italian is, like the licensing of *wh*-phrases, accomplished sometimes by (covert) phrasal movement to the licenser, and sometimes by feature movement. Suggestive evidence for this hypothesis comes from the fact that long-distance licensing of an NPI over an intervener (such as a closer instance of negation) obeys island conditions that other instances of licensing do not, as noted by Kurata (1991). For example, licensing of an NPI by the nearest negation (or other licenser) does not display any subject/nonsubject asymmetry.

(i) a. John doesn't think that Mary loves anyone.
    b. John doesn't think that anyone loves Mary.

When an NPI has a choice between a nearer licenser and a further licenser, the facts are different. In (ii) the embedded object *anyone* may be licensed either by *impossible* in the middle clause or by negation in the higher clause. Kurata paraphrases the two readings as shown.

(ii) I don't believe it to be impossible that John saw anyone.
    Narrow scope: 'I believe it is possible that John saw at least one person.'
    Wide scope: 'I believe of each person that it is possible that John saw that person.'

By contrast, in (iii) the embedded subject *anyone* has only a reading in which it is licensed by the nearest instance of negation (the negative predicate *impossible*).

(iii) I don't believe it to be impossible that anyone saw John.
    Narrow scope: 'I believe it possible that at least one person saw John.'
    Wide scope: *'I believe of each person that it is possible that that person saw John.'

Guerzoni suggests that the only way to allow an NPI to have wider scope than an intervening negation is through covert phrasal movement (a suggestion supported by evidence from ACD) to a position close to the licenser of the NPI (perhaps [Spec, NegP]). It is this type of movement, she suggests, that displays subject/object asymmetries (as argued extensively in work of the 1980s; see, e.g., Kayne 1984). When scope is not assigned across an intervener, the licensing relation can be established by feature movement, with no subject/object asymmetry—as seen in (i).

References

Aoun, Joseph, Norbert Hornstein, David Lightfoot, and Amy Weinberg. 1987. Two types of locality. *Linguistic Inquiry* 18, 537–578.

Aoun, Joseph, Norbert Hornstein, and Dominique Sportiche. 1981. Aspects of wide scope quantification. *Journal of Linguistic Research* 1, 67–95.

Aoun, Joseph, and Yen-hui Audrey Li. 1993a. *Wh*-elements in situ: Syntax or LF? *Linguistic Inquiry* 24, 199–238.

Aoun, Joseph, and Yen-hui Audrey Li. 1993b. On some differences between Chinese and Japanese *wh*-elements. *Linguistic Inquiry* 24, 365–372.

Baltin, Mark. 1987. Do antecedent-contained deletions exist? *Linguistic Inquiry* 18, 579–595.

Barbosa, Pilar, Danny Fox, Paul Hagstrom, Martha McGinnis, and David Pesetsky, eds. 1998. *Is the best good enough?* Cambridge, Mass.: MIT Press and MITWPL.

Barss, Andrew. To appear. Minimalism and asymmetric *wh*-interpretation. In Roger Martin, David Michaels, and Juan Uriagereka, eds., *Step by step: Essays in honor of Howard Lasnik*. Cambridge, Mass.: MIT Press.

Beck, Sigrid. 1996. Quantified structures as barriers for LF movement. *Natural Language Semantics* 4, 1–56.

Beck, Sigrid, and Shin-Sook Kim. 1996. On *wh*- and operator scope in Korean. *Journal of East Asian Linguistics* 6, 339–384.

Besten, Hans den. 1983. On the interaction of root transformations and lexical deletive rules. In Werner Abraham, ed., *On the formal syntax of the West-germania*. Amsterdam: John Benjamins.

Billings, Loren, and Catherine Rudin. 1994. Optimality and superiority: A new approach to overt multiple-*wh* ordering. In Jindřich Toman, ed., *Proceedings of FASL 3: The College Park Meeting*. Ann Arbor, Mich.: Michigan Slavic Publications.

Bobaljik, Jonathan. 1995. Morphosyntax: The syntax of verbal inflection. Doctoral dissertation, MIT, Cambridge, Mass.

Boeckx, Cedric. 1999a. Decomposing French questions. In Jim Alexander, Na-Rae Han, and Michelle Minnick Fox, eds., *UPenn working papers in linguistics 6*. PWPL, Penn Linguistics Club, University of Pennsylvania, Philadelphia.

Boeckx, Cedric. 1999b. Properties of French questions. Ms., University of Connecticut, Storrs.

Bošković, Željko. 1995. On certain violations of the Superiority Condition, AgrO, and economy of derivation. *Journal of Linguistics* 33, 227–254.

Bošković, Željko. 1998. Multiple *wh*-fronting and economy of derivation. In Emily Curtis, James Lyle, and Gabriel Webster, eds., *Proceedings of the 16th West Coast Conference on Formal Linguistics*. Stanford, Calif.: CSLI Publications. [Distributed by Cambridge University Press.]

Bošković, Željko. 1999. On multiple feature checking: Multiple *wh*-fronting and multiple head movement. In Samuel David Epstein and Norbert Hornstein, eds., *Working minimalism*. Cambridge, Mass.: MIT Press.

Bošković, Željko. To appear. Sometimes in [Spec, CP], sometimes in situ. In Roger Martin, David Michaels, and Juan Uriagereka, eds., *Step by step: Essays in honor of Howard Lasnik*. Cambridge, Mass.: MIT Press.

Bouton, Lawrence F. 1970. Antecedent-contained pro-forms. In *Papers from the Sixth Regional Meeting, Chicago Linguistic Society*. Chicago Linguistic Society, University of Chicago, Chicago, Ill.

Brody, Michael. 1995. *Lexico-Logical Form*. Cambridge, Mass.: MIT Press.

Brody, Michael. 1997. Perfect chains. In Liliane Haegeman, ed., *Handbook of syntax*. Dordrecht: Kluwer.

Büring, Daniel. 1994. The dark side of *wh*-movement. *Linguistische Berichte* 149, 56–74.

Chang, Lisa. 1997. *Wh*-in-situ phenomena in French. Doctoral dissertation, University of British Columbia, Vancouver.

Cheng, Lisa. 1991. On the typology of *wh*-questions. Doctoral dissertation, MIT, Cambridge, Mass. [Reprinted, New York: Garland, 1997.]

Cheng, Lisa. 1997. "Partial" *wh*-movement. In Luther Chen-Sheng Liu and Kazue Takeda, eds., *UCI working papers in linguistics 3*. Department of Linguistics, University of California, Irvine.

Cheng, Lisa. To appear. Moving just the feature. In Uli Lutz, Gereon Müller, and Arnim von Stechow, eds., *Wh-scope marking*. Amsterdam: John Benjamins.

Chierchia, Gennaro. 1993. Questions with quantifiers. *Natural Language Semantics* 1, 181–234.

Chomsky, Noam. 1973. Conditions on transformations. In Stephen Anderson and Paul Kiparsky, eds., *A festschrift for Morris Halle*. New York: Holt, Rinehart and Winston.

Chomsky, Noam. 1976. Conditions on rules of grammar. *Linguistic Analysis* 2, 303–351. [Reprinted in *Essays on form and interpretation*. New York: Elsevier North-Holland, 1977.]

Chomsky, Noam. 1981. *Lectures on government and binding*. Dordrecht: Foris. [Reprinted, Dordrecht: Mouton de Gruyter, 1993.]

Chomsky, Noam. 1986a. *Barriers*. Cambridge, Mass.: MIT Press.

Chomsky, Noam. 1986b. *Knowledge of language: Its nature, origins, and use*. New York: Praeger.

Chomsky, Noam. 1991. Some notes on economy of derivation and representation. In Robert Freidin, ed., *Principles and parameters in comparative grammar*. Cambridge, Mass.: MIT Press. [Also published in Noam Chomsky, *The Minimalist Program*. Cambridge, Mass.: MIT Press, 1995.]

Chomsky, Noam. 1993. A minimalist program for linguistic theory. In Kenneth Hale and Samuel Jay Keyser, eds., *The view from Building 20*. Cambridge, Mass.: MIT Press. [Also published in Noam Chomsky, *The Minimalist Program*. Cambridge, Mass.: MIT Press, 1995.]

Chomsky, Noam. 1995. Categories and transformations. In *The Minimalist Program*. Cambridge, Mass.: MIT Press.

Chomsky, Noam. 1998. Minimalist inquiries: The framework. (MIT Occasional Papers in Linguistics 15.) MITWPL, Department of Linguistics and Philosophy, MIT, Cambridge, Mass. [To appear in Roger Martin, David Michaels, and Juan Uriagereka, eds., *Step by step: Essays in honor of Howard Lasnik*. Cambridge, Mass.: MIT Press.]

Chomsky, Noam, and Howard Lasnik. 1977. Filters and control. *Linguistic Inquiry* 8, 425–504.

Chung, Sandra, and James McCloskey. 1983. On the interpretation of certain island facts in GPSG. *Linguistic Inquiry* 14, 704–713.

Cole, Peter, and Gabriella Hermon. 1998. The typology of *wh* movement. *Syntax* 1, 221–258.

Comorovski, Ileana. 1996. *Interrogative phrases and the syntax-semantics interface*. Kluwer: Dordrecht.

Diesing, Molly. 1992. *Indefinites*. Cambridge, Mass.: MIT Press.

Engdahl, Elisabet. 1980. The syntax and semantics of questions in Swedish. Doctoral dissertation, University of Massachusetts, Amherst.

Engel, Ulrich. 1972. *Regeln zur Satzgliedfolge: Zur Stellung der Elemente im einfachen Verbalsatz*. Düsseldorf: Schwann.

Fanselow, Gisbert. 1990. Scrambling as NP-movement. In Günther Grewendorf and Wolfgang Sternefeld, eds., *Scrambling and barriers*. Amsterdam: John Benjamins.

Fanselow, Gisbert. 1991. Minimale Syntax. Habilitation thesis, University of Passau.

Fanselow, Gisbert. 1997. Minimal Link effects in German (and other languages). Ms., University of Potsdam. [Related 1996 handout at http://www.ling.uni-potsdam.de/~fanselow/mlc.htm]

Fiengo, Robert. 1998. How to ask multiple questions—some simple ways: A footnote to Austin. Ms., Queens College and the Graduate Center of CUNY, New York.

Fiengo, Robert, and Robert May. 1994. *Indices and identity*. Cambridge, Mass.: MIT Press.

Fox, Danny. 1995. Condition C effects in ACD. In Rob Pensalfini and Hiroyuki Ura, eds., *Papers on minimalist syntax*. (MIT Working Papers in Linguistics 27.) MITWPL, Department of Linguistics and Philosophy, MIT, Cambridge, Mass.

Fox, Danny. 1998. Economy and semantic interpretation: A study of scope and variable binding. Doctoral dissertation, MIT, Cambridge, Mass.

Gazdar, Gerald. 1981. Unbounded dependencies and coordinate structure. *Linguistic Inquiry* 12, 155–184.

Gazdar, Gerald, Ewan Klein, Geoffrey Pullum, and Ivan Sag. 1985. *Generalized Phrase Structure Grammar*. Cambridge, Mass.: Harvard University Press.

George, Leland. 1980. Analogical generalization in natural language syntax. Doctoral dissertation, MIT, Cambridge, Mass.

Grewendorf, Günther, and Wolfgang Sternefeld. 1990. Scrambling theories. In Günther Grewendorf and Wolfgang Sternefeld, eds., *Scrambling and barriers*. Amsterdam: John Benjamins.

Grimshaw, Jane. 1997. Projection, heads, and optimality. *Linguistic Inquiry* 28, 363–422.

Groat, Erich, and John O'Neil. 1996. Spell-out at the LF interface. In Werner Abraham, Samuel D. Epstein, Höskuldur Thráinsson, and Jan-Wouter Zwart, eds., *Minimal ideas*. Amsterdam: John Benjamins.

Grohmann, Kleanthes. 1998. Syntactic inquiries into discourse restrictions on multiple interrogatives. Ms., University of Maryland, College Park.

Guerzoni, Elena. 1999. Phrasal and feature movement: Syntactic conditions on NPI licensing. Ms., MIT, Cambridge, Mass.

Hagstrom, Paul. 1998. Decomposing questions. Doctoral dissertation, MIT, Cambridge, Mass.

Haider, Hubert. 1986. Affect α: A reply to Lasnik and Saito, "On the nature of proper government." *Linguistic Inquiry* 17, 113–125.

Haider, Hubert. 2000. Towards a superior account of Superiority. In Uli Lutz, Gereon Müller, and Arnim von Stechow, eds., *Wh*-scope marking. Amsterdam: John Benjamins.

Hankamer, Jorge. 1974. On WH indexing. In Ellen Kaisse and Jorge Hankamer, eds., *Papers from the Fifth Annual Meeting of the North Eastern Linguistic Society*. Department of Linguistics, Harvard University, Cambridge, Mass.

Hankamer, Jorge, and Ivan Sag. 1976. Deep and surface anaphora. *Linguistic Inquiry* 7, 391–428.

Hasegawa, Nobuko. 1994. Economy of derivation and A′-movement in Japanese. In Masaru Nakamura, ed. *Current Topics in English and Japanese*. Tokyo: Hituzi Syobo.

Hoji, Hajime. 1985. Logical Form constraints and configurational structures in Japanese. Doctoral dissertation, University of Washington, Seattle.

Honcoop, Martin. 1998. *Dynamic excursions on weak islands*. The Hague: Holland Academic Graphics.

Hornstein, Norbert. 1994. An argument for minimalism: The case of antecedent-contained deletion. *Linguistic Inquiry* 25, 455–480.

Hornstein, Norbert. 1995. *Logical Form: From GB to minimalism*. Cambridge, Mass.: Blackwell.

Huang, C.-T. James. 1981. Move *wh* in a language without *wh* movement. *The Linguistic Review* 1, 369–416.

Huang, C.-T. James. 1982. Logical relations in Chinese and the theory of grammar. Doctoral dissertation, MIT, Cambridge, Mass. [Reprinted, New York: Garland, 1998.]

Johnson, Kyle. 1992. Object positions. *Natural Language & Linguistic Theory* 9, 577–636.

Johnson, Kyle, and Satoshi Tomioka. 1997. Lowering and mid-size clauses. Ms., University of Massachusetts, Amherst, and University of California, San Diego.

Kayne, Richard. 1983. Connectedness. *Linguistic Inquiry* 14, 223–249. [Reprinted in Kayne 1984.]

Kayne, Richard. 1984. *Connectedness and binary branching*. Dordrecht: Foris.

Kayne, Richard. 1994. *The antisymmetry of syntax*. Cambridge, Mass.: MIT Press.

Kayne, Richard. 1998. Overt vs. covert movement. Ms., New York University.

Kennedy, Christopher. 1997. Antecedent-contained deletion and the syntax of quantification. *Linguistic Inquiry* 28, 662–688.

É. Kiss, Katalin. 1986. Against the LF-movement of WH-phrases. Ms., Hungarian Academy of Sciences, Budapest.

Koizumi, Masatoshi. 1995. Phrase structure in minimalist syntax. Doctoral dissertation, MIT, Cambridge, Mass.

Koot, Hans van de. 1988. The vacuous movement hypothesis, superiority and the ECP. In Ger de Haan and Wim Zonneveld, eds., *Formal parameters of generative grammar IV: Yearbook 1988*. Dordrecht: ICG Printing.

Koster, Jan. 1987. *Domains and dynasties*. Dordrecht: Foris.

Kuno, Susumu. 1982. The focus of the question and the focus of the answer. In Robinson Schneider, Kevin Tuite, and Robert Chametzky, eds., *Papers from the Parasession on Nondeclaratives*. Chicago Linguistic Society, University of Chicago, Chicago, Ill.

Kuno, Susumu, and Jane J. Robinson. 1972. Multiple wh questions. *Linguistic Inquiry* 3, 463–487.

Kurata, Kiyoshi. 1991. The syntax of dependent elements. Doctoral dissertation, University of Massachusetts, Amherst.

Larson, Richard, Marcel den Dikken, and Peter Ludlow. 1997. Intensional transitive verbs and abstract clausal complementation. Ms., SUNY at Stony Brook.

Larson, Richard, and Robert May. 1990. Antecedent containment or vacuous movement: Reply to Baltin. *Linguistic Inquiry* 21, 103–122.

Lasnik, Howard. 1993. Lectures on Minimalist syntax. (Occasional Papers 1.) Department of Linguistics, University of Connecticut, Storrs. [Distributed by MITWPL, Department of Linguistics and Philosophy, MIT, Cambridge, Mass.]

Lasnik, Howard. 1999. *Minimalist analysis.* Oxford: Blackwell.

Lasnik, Howard, and Mamoru Saito. 1984. On the nature of proper government. *Linguistic Inquiry* 15, 235–290.

Legendre, Géraldine, Paul Smolensky, and Colin Wilson. 1998. When is less more? Faithfulness and minimal links in wh-chains. In Pilar Barbosa, Danny Fox, Paul Hagstrom, Martha McGinnis, and David Pesetsky, eds., *Is the best good enough?* Cambridge, Mass.: MIT Press and MITWPL.

Longobardi, Giuseppe. 1986. L'estrazione dalle isole e lo scope dei sintagmi quantificati. In K. Lichem, E. Mara, and S. Knaller, eds., *Parallela 2: Atti del terzo Incontro Italo-Austriaco di Linguisti.* Tübingen: Gunter Narr.

Longobardi, Giuseppe. 1991. In defense of the correspondence hypothesis: Island effects and parasitic constructions in Logical Form. In C.-T. James Huang and Robert May, eds., *Logical structure and linguistic structure.* Dordrecht: Kluwer.

Mahajan, Anoop. 1990. The A/A' distinction and movement theory. Doctoral dissertation, MIT, Cambridge, Mass.

May, Robert. 1977. The grammar of quantification. Doctoral dissertation, MIT, Cambridge, Mass.

May, Robert. 1985. *Logical Form.* Cambridge, Mass.: MIT Press.

McCloskey, James. 2000. Quantifier float and *wh*-movement in an Irish English. *Linguistic Inquiry* 31, 57–84

Miyagawa, Shigeru. 1997. Class handout, MIT, Cambridge, Mass.

Miyagawa, Shigeru. 1998. *WH* chains and quantifier induced barriers. Ms., MIT, Cambridge, Mass.

Müller, Gereon. 1995. *A-bar syntax: A study in movement types.* Berlin: Mouton de Gruyter.

Müller, Gereon. 1996. A constraint on remnant movement. *Natural Language & Linguistic Theory* 14, 355–407.

Müller, Gereon. 1998. Order preservation, parallel movement, and the emergence of the unmarked. Ms., Universität Stuttgart. [ftp://ruccs.rutgers.edu/pub/OT/TEXTS/archive/275-0798/275-07982.pdf]

Müller, Gereon, and Wolfgang Sternefeld. 1993. Improper movement and unambiguous binding. *Linguistic Inquiry* 24, 461–507.

Nunes, Jairo. 1995. The copy theory of movement and linearization of chains in the Minimalist Program. Doctoral dissertation, University of Connecticut, Storrs.

Obenauer, Hans-Georg. 1984. On the identification of empty categories. *The Linguistic Review* 4, 153–202.

Ochi, Masao. 1998. Move or Attract? In Emily Curtis, James Lyle, and Gabriel Webster, eds., *Proceedings of the 16th West Coast Conference on Formal Linguistics*. Stanford, Calif.: CSLI Publications. [Distributed by Cambridge University Press.]

Perlmutter, David. 1972. Evidence for shadow pronouns in French relativization. In P. Peranteau, J. Levi, and G. Phares, eds., *The Chicago which hunt: Papers from the Relative Clause Festival*. Chicago Linguistic Society, University of Chicago, Chicago, Ill.

Pesetsky, David. 1982. Paths and categories. Doctoral dissertation, MIT, Cambridge, Mass.

Pesetsky, David. 1987. *Wh*-in-situ: Movement and unselective binding. In Eric Reuland and Alice ter Meulen, eds., *The representation of (in)definiteness*. Cambridge, Mass.: MIT Press.

Pesetsky, David. 1989. Language-particular rules and the Earliness Principle. Ms., MIT, Cambridge, Mass.

Pesetsky, David. 1997. Optimality Theory and syntax: Movement and pronunciation. In Diana Archangeli and D. Terence Langendoen, eds., *Optimality Theory: An overview*. Oxford: Blackwell.

Pesetsky, David. 1998. Some optimality principles of sentence pronunciation. In Pilar Barbosa, Danny Fox, Paul Hagstrom, Martha McGinnis, and David Pesetsky, eds., *Is the best good enough?* Cambridge, Mass.: MIT Press and MITWPL.

Pollard, Carl, and Ivan A. Sag. 1994. *Head-Driven Phrase Structure Grammar*. Chicago: University of Chicago Press.

Prince, Alan, and Paul Smolensky. 1993. Optimality Theory: Constraint interaction in generative grammar. Technical Report 2, Rutgers University Center for Cognitive Science, Piscataway, N. J. [To appear, Cambridge, Mass.: MIT Press.]

Reinhart, Tanya. 1997. Quantifier scope: How labor is divided between QR and choice functions. *Linguistics and Philosophy* 20, 335–397.

Richards, Norvin. 1997. What moves where in which language? Doctoral dissertation, MIT, Cambridge, Mass.

Rizzi, Luigi. 1990. *Relativized Minimality*. Cambridge, Mass.: MIT Press.

Ross, John R. 1967. Constraints on variables in syntax. Doctoral dissertation, MIT, Cambridge, Mass.

Rudin, Catherine. 1985. *Aspects of Bulgarian syntax: Complementizers and wh constructions*. Columbus, Ohio: Slavica.

Rudin, Catherine. 1988. On multiple questions and multiple WH fronting. *Natural Language & Linguistic Theory* 6, 445–502.

Sag, Ivan. 1976. Deletion and Logical Form. Doctoral dissertation, MIT, Cambridge, Mass.

Saito, Mamoru. 1992. Long distance scrambling in Japanese. *Journal of East Asian Linguistics* 1, 69–118.

Saito, Mamoru. 1994. Additional *wh*-effects and the adjunction site theory. *Journal of East Asian Linguistics* 3, 195–240.

Sauerland, Uli. 1996. The interpretability of scrambling. In Masa Koizumi, Masayuki Oichi, and Uli Sauerland, eds., *Formal Approaches to Japanese Linguistics 2*. (MIT Working Papers in Linguistics 29.) MITWPL, Department of Linguistics and Philosophy, MIT, Cambridge, Mass.

Sauerland, Uli. 1998a. Erasability and interpretation. Ms., Kanda University, Makuhari Kaihin, Japan.

Sauerland, Uli. 1998b. The meaning of chains. Doctoral dissertation, MIT, Cambridge, Mass.

Stjepanović, Sandra. 1998. On the placement of Serbo-Croatian clitics: Evidence from VP-ellipsis. *Linguistic Inquiry* 29, 513–515.

Takahashi, Daiko. 1993. Movement of *wh*-phrases in Japanese. *Natural Language & Linguistic Theory* 11, 655–678.

Takahashi, Daiko. 1994. Minimality of movement. Doctoral dissertation, University of Connecticut, Storrs.

Tanaka, Hidekazu. 1999. Conditions on Logical Form derivations and representations. Doctoral dissertation, McGill University, Montreal, Que.

Tsai, Wei-Tien Dylan. 1994. On nominal islands and LF extraction in Chinese. *Natural Language & Linguistic Theory* 12, 121–175.

Ura, Hiroyuki. 1996. Multiple feature checking: A theory of grammatical function splitting. Doctoral dissertation, MIT, Cambridge, Mass.

Wachowicz, Krzystina. 1974. Against the universality of a single WH-question movement. *Foundations of Language* 11, 155–166.

Watanabe, Akira. 1992. Subjacency and S-Structure movement of *wh*-in-situ. *Journal of East Asian Linguistics* 1, 255–291.

Webelhuth, Gert. 1988. Syntactic saturation phenomena and the modern Germanic languages. Doctoral dissertation, University of Massachusetts, Amherst.

Wilder, Chris. 1999. Right node raising and the LCA. In Sonya Bird, Andrew Carnie, and Peter Norquest, eds., *Proceedings of the 19th West Coast Conference on Formal Linguistics*. Stanford, Calif.: CSLI Publications. [Distributed by Cambridge University Press.]

Wiltschko, Martina. 1997. D-linking, scrambling and superiority in German. In Werner Abraham, ed., *Groninger Arbeiten zur germanistischen Linguistik 41*. Germanistisch Instituut, Rijksuniversiteit Groningen.

Wurmbrand, Susanne. 1998. Infinitives. Doctoral dissertation, MIT, Cambridge, Mass.

Index